How to Move to Kona

JULIE ZIEMELIS

The Larry Czerwonka Company, LLC
Hilo, Hawai'i

First Edition — November 2014

This book is set in 12-point Garamond

Published by: The Larry Czerwonka Company, LLC
http://thelarryczerwonkacompany.com

Printed in the United States of America

ISBN: 0692327525
ISBN-13: 978-0692327524

This book is dedicated to my husband, Eric Ziemelis, and my two children, Caylin and Devin. They have been my fellow adventurers, cockroach swatters, 365Kona supporters, and creators of a life well lived.

Contents

Acknowledgements

Every story has a story behind it. My story started out as an adventure and was magnified with the use of social media. By learning how to build a blog on WordPress to write my story, and building a Facebook business page to share that story, along with hundreds of photos of the Big Island, this book is now in your hands or on your screen.

There are a few key people I would like to thank who helped make this lifelong dream of becoming a published author happen:

First to my editor, Beth Dunnington, who heard me read my stories aloud at her Women's Writing Workshop over the past six months and encouraged me to post them. I told her I was working on a guide about moving to Kona, and she told me I needed an editor. She became more than an editor. She became my coach when I worried about how the book would be received by island residents and she was my cheerleader to keep writing deeper with more informative chapters. Mahalo nui loa, Beth.

Thanks goes to my web partner, Scott Schang, for building out my 365Kona site, and adding analytics so I could see the volume of traffic from people searching for information about moving to the Big Island. That gave me the impetus to write blog posts addressing those questions and concerns. He also helped me to become a better blogger, which helped me find consulting jobs here in Hawai'i!

To my family, and especially my husband, Eric, who took the leap of faith with me in moving to the island, without a guidebook, to set off on an adventure of a lifetime. He helped me discover the landscape, culture, and people of Hawai'i.

1

Thanks to my mother, who passed away while I was writing this book. She always thought I could do anything I set my mind to. I love that she had a chance to come visit us in Kona and swim with the turtles. I know she is proud that I wrote a book that will help many people make their decision to live a life that is bold.

To my Facebook fans and friends, who used the "like" button consistently enough to keep me posting almost daily, and kept me out there exploring and discovering all the cool activities, beaches, forests, restaurants, and fun things to do in Hawai'i. My husband says we are never alone on our activities as we take hundreds of people with us virtually, thanks to Facebook!

To my business coach, Stephanie Beeby, In Flow CEO, for coaching me, since 2012, to share my insights, knowledge, and passion through a book/webinar. I finally did it. Thanks, Stephanie.

To my social friends who taught me how to use the tools to share my stories, and for online encouragement along the way—Stacey Harmon, Harmon Enterprises; Katie Lance, Katie Lance Consulting; Kelly Mitchell, AgentCaffeine; Melissa Arianna Case; Amie Chilson; Jim Walberg; Mark Gross.

To the local friends I mention throughout this book, and to those who added their thoughts and experiences to the mix: John Philips, Colin Jevens, Lisa Pegg, Denise Laitenen, Cjay Moongarden, Laurie Mattos, Jean Mabry, Lance Owens, Delania Branham, Maya Cole, Beth Dunnington, Carole Gruskin, Ilona Honig, Lynn Pinault, Ron Lloyd, Norman Bezona, Greg Colden, and Una Greenway.

To my publisher, Larry Czerwonka, who created a unique publishing company to help island writers get their books out into the world. Thank you for your help in publishing and marketing this book!

Most of all, I want to thank YOU for buying this book. Be sure to join me on my website, 365Kona.com, and my "365 Things To Do in Kona" Facebook page for cool things to do. Keep an eye out for my events for newcomers to Kona to meet new friends. Mahalo nui loa!

Introduction

E Komo Mai: Welcome and Aloha!

In 1866 Mark Twain came on assignment from *The Sacramento Union* newspaper to spend a week writing about what he experienced in the islands. His response, "I went to Maui to stay a week and remained five. I had a jolly time. I would not have fooled away any of it writing letters under any consideration whatever."

Personally, I came to stay for a year and then had to play, work, and explore Kona for nine years before I could write this book.

I came to Kona in 2005 to live here for just a year with my husband and two small children. But Hawai'i has a way of getting into your soul and binding your spirit. After going back to the Silicon Valley in 2006 when our year was up, my family and I came back for several summers and finally decided to leave the mainland far behind (2,313 miles to be exact), and in the summer of 2010 we made Kona our home. I immediately created the Facebook page "365 Things To Do In Kona" and started a blog at 365Kona.com. Like Twain, I was smitten with what I found here—the culture, the beauty of the island, the adventures, and the people. I did not set out to write a book when I started blogging, but after writing about Kona and the Big Island for four years, people started writing to me and asking me questions about what it was like to live here, what tips could I share so they could make Hawai'i their home, and what would I have done differently so they could avoid the mishaps we encountered on our new island home. After personally answering these questions via email and Facebook for the past few years, and having my blog post, "Why the Big Island Is a Terrible Place to Live" featured on the front page of the *Huffington Post*, I wanted to share my experience in a resource guide. This book is for the brave souls willing to cast off their lives on the mainland (or on other islands) to come find a new life in Kona.

A friend who is moving here soon was talking with me about the mission of this book. "These people know about the high cost of living, they know it's hard to find a job, and still they want to come. What can you tell them?" he asked. I can tell them plenty, actually, and thus I wrote this guide—not to entice, but to provide resources and tips that I wish someone would have shared with me before I arrived with my family at KOA with no friends, no job or connections, nor any idea about the land I was about to call my home.

Before I arrived here, I had heard of the Hawaiian term *haole*, and have spent the past four years learning how to NOT be the negative definition of *haole*, but rather the positive one, which basically means foreigner. Yes, I am a foreigner, but like others before me, I love this island and wish to spread the Aloha Spirit while assisting others to understand and take care of this magical place. If you feel a connection of to the island, feel compelled to be here, feel you are "at home" when you visit and long for it while you are away, or if you simply want to have the adventure of your life, then my goal is to help you find your way. This book will give you a road map for getting in the door, but it will be your tenacity, desire, and will to stay here that will ultimately guide your success as a resident.

Hawai'i has a way of grabbing your imagination, your soul, and your spirit, and as Mark Twain said, you will "be haunted by it." You have a chance, right now, as you read this book, to decide if you will be haunted or rewarded, bound to your stuff and your life off the island, or make a new life and take a risk. The biggest risk in life is not to take one, right? But if you do, I want you to see the caution cones with your eyes fully open. Okay? Read on, then.

Mark Twain's Letters (1866)

"No alien land in all the world has any deep strong charm for me but one, no other land could so longingly and so beseechingly haunt me, sleeping and waking, through half a lifetime, as that one has done. Other things leave me, but it abides; other things change, but it remains the same. For me its balmy airs are always blowing, its summer seas flashing in the sun; the pulsing of its surf beat is in my ear; I can see its garland crags, its leaping cascades, its plumy palms drowsing by the shore, its remote summits floating like islands above the cloud wrack; I can feel the spirit of its woodland solitudes, I can hear the splash of its brooks; in my nostrils still lives the breath of flowers that perished twenty years ago."

Getting

Here

Chapter One

Hawaiian Principles for Living You Should Know Before Arriving

Coming to live in Hawai'i is like moving to a foreign land. If you understand this fact, you will create your approach to moving a bit differently. There is definitely a culture here that needs to be learned, recognized, and respected in order for you to settle in successfully.

There is one word you may hear in Hawai'i that you may not like: *haole*. It's pronounced HOWLIE. You may know it as a derogatory slang word for white people. In researching the origins of this word, I found a few. One states that the Hawaiians, observing the European's white skin, thought they were ghosts. The other story states that foreigners did not know or use the *honi* (a Polynesian greeting by touching nose-to-nose, inhaling, or sharing each other's breath), and so the foreigners were described as without breath.

In 1944, Hawaiian scholar Charles Kenn wrote, "In the primary and esoteric meaning, *haole* indicates a race that has no relation to one's own; an outsider, one who does not conform to the mores of the group; one that is void of the life element because of inattention to natural laws which make for the goodness in man."[1]

Europeans greeted each other with a handshake, which originated as a way to show they did not have a weapon. A more personal and friendly greeting than a handshake still persists today. When you greet

9

someone in Hawai'i, you hug them and kiss them on the cheek. Sticking your hand out is a dead giveaway that you are a mainlander.

Back to *haole*, the euphemism that many use as another form of "you don't belong here" or "you don't know our culture." This can be avoided in most instances by not acting like you just got off the boat in a foreign country and did not take the time to learn anything about the land you are about to call home. Most native Hawaiians and old time residents alike expect you to have respect for them and the culture. You will get along well if you remember this.

When I first arrived at the Kona Airport, and I am ashamed to admit this, I was a *haole* because I did not bring any knowledge of Hawaiian culture with me. I just moved here. During the first few months of living here, I often received strange looks, the kind you get when you are unintentionally committing some level of cultural faux pas. Most frequently, I would get these looks from parents at the school where we chose to enroll my daughter. I would show up in my Silicon Valley outfits, offer handshakes to those I was greeting, and had to ask numerous times about Hawaiian words and phrases they were using. Making it worse, in 2005 the school was a Waldorf school, which was very "organic." Coming from Silicon Valley, I stepped into a double world of culture shock.

My bull in a china shop antics continued with my butchering the pronunciation of Hawaiian towns and street names. Try saying, "Napo'opo'o Road" and "Queen Kaahumanu Highway." (One of the fastest ways to offend just about any resident of Hawai'i is to not even try to say the towns or street names correctly.) I also did not know the basic Hawaiian words that find their way into the general lexicon of people who live here, making me a target of stink eye at gatherings. Let me save you from this fate!

First of all, before you come, do yourself a favor and learn about the rich history of the Hawaiian culture and some basic words that everyone uses. If you did not know, James A. Michener's *Hawaii* is a great novel, but it's not the definitive book on Hawaiian history. I would suggest *Lost Kingdom: Hawaii's Last Queen, the Sugar Kings and American's First Imperial Adventure* by Julia Flynn Siler.

http://bit.ly/LostKingdom

An early trip to the Hulihee Palace in downtown Kona will help bring history to life by the wonderful docents there who tell the stories of King Kamehameha and his family.

For the pronunciation of common words, check out this site to actually hear the words the way they are SUPPOSED to be pronounced:

http://bit.ly/CommonHawaiianWords

Here's a funny/useful blog post about common words you will hear when you spend some time talking to people in Hawai'i:

http://bit.ly/WordsToLearn

Here are some of the words and phrases I find in use daily:

'Āina. The Land.

Aloha. Love, affection, compassion, mercy, sympathy, pity, kindness. [Discover the meaning of Aloha and you will see a deeper side to the culture and perhaps **understand** why you feel drawn here. This is my personal take on the word *aloha*:

    Alo. Meaning "sharing" or "in the present."

    Oha. Meaning "joyous affection, joy."

    Ha. Meaning "life energy, life, breath."

    I translate this as, "The joyful sharing of life energy in the present" or simply "Joyfully sharing life."

[Read the book *The Deeper Meaning of Aloha* by Curby Rule. It's both fascinating and provides insight and respect for the word. http://bit.ly/DeeperMeaningAloha]

E Komo Mai. Welcome.

Heiau. A place of worship.

Keiki. Children.

Kōkua. Help, aid.

Kuleana. Responsibility.

Kumu. Teacher.

Kupuna. Ancestor, grandparent.

Mahalo nui loa. Thank you very much.

Makai. Towards the sea {a common way to tell direction}.

Mauka. Inland {a common way to tell direction}.

Pau. Finished {also used in *pau hana* (time after work, happy hour)}.

Pono. Righteous.

Puka. Hole {this word can be used when discussing filling in a place within a line of kids or a place in the center courtyard, etc.}.

There are words that are more spiritually significant that you may not speak every day, but you should know enough to remember that you are not just a physical resident of Hawai'i, you are a spiritual one as well.

Ho'oponopono. To make right {essentially, it means to make it right with the ancestors, or to make right with the people with whom you have relationships}. [I first heard this used when I was told to go back with an offering of flowers and forgiveness for unknowingly walking all over a hidden Hawaiian village.]

Huaka'i pō. Night marchers, ghosts of ancient Hawaiian warriors. [If you are a fan of the supernatural, you should dig into this more. I wrote a post called "Haunted Hawai'i" about some of the *happenings* on the islands. I do believe if you hear about something enough times from a variety of different people who have been here a long time . . . well . . . http://bit.ly/Haunted.]

Kapu. Taboo, prohibition, forbidden. [If you see this sign at the base of a trail, garden, or historical site, DO NOT ENTER. If you are sensitive to such things, you can actually feel the energy change in these areas. I felt it when I was about to climb the steps of a *heiau* (an ancient place of worship) that had been used for human sacrifice. Seriously, heed this sign out of respect for the culture.]

Mana. Supernatural or divine power {your *mana* is also known as your life force or spirit}.

I believe that, as a resident of the island, connecting to the land and the spirit of the island is imperative. There are wonderful and helpful concepts to know so you can achieve a deeper respect for your new island home.

"*Aloha 'āina* means to love and respect the land, make it yours, and claim stewardship for it.

Malama 'āina means to care for and nurture the land so it can give back all we need to sustain life for our future generations and ourselves.

An *ahupua'a* is an ancient concept of resource use and management based on families living in a division of land that connects the mountains to the reefs and the sea."

— Puanani Rogers, Team Leader for the Ho'okipa Network

Another Word on Local Culture: Cars and Clothes

Ask Kona residents, and you will find that the folks who live here do not display wealth. This was another culture shock we adjusted to in a good way!

People don't ask you what kind of a car you drive or what you do for a living to size you up and figure out how much money you make. Ostentatious displays of wealth are looked down upon, and unless you are supporting a local charity by raising a paddle at a live auction, keep your worth to yourself. Gentlemen of all classes wear shorts, sandals, and Aloha shirts. Women wear sundresses, shorts and tank tops, or blouses. It's okay to spend just about your entire day doing errands in gym wear. Ponytails and baseball caps are refreshing ways to avoid doing your hair every day if you don't have to go into the office. Everyone wears *slippahs* (flip flops).

Maseratis and Ferraris are not found here. Not just because they don't fit in, but the salt from the ocean air will kill expensive sports cars and there are no parts on the island. (See Chapter 8 – Resource Guide pg. 41.) What you wear and drive here is based on comfort, functionality, and practicality. I have a friend who brought over all her fancy shoes from Seattle and finds little excuse to wear most of them. This lack of wealth display is refreshing coming from a "keeping up with the Jones/Kardashians" mainland city environment. No one will be impressed if you flash your Rolex, Gucci purse, or Laboutins. You probably would not be moving here if you cared about that stuff anyway, right?

Making new friends is about being yourself, not your showing off your stuff. Bring a few nice clothes for taking your friends to the resorts, special events, and going back to the mainland for visits. Gentlemen should be aware that long pants are required to go to court and funerals. Here's hoping that you can avoid both of these types of events.

notes

1. Haole - Wikipedia, the free encyclopedia, http://en.wikipedia.org/wiki/Haole (accessed October 1, 2014).

Chapter Two
Risks and Realities of Paradise

When you live on a volcanic island, you immediately sign up for some risks that people on the mainland do not face. The Hawaiian Islands have a number of natural disasters that not only CAN strike, but DO! We found out that Hawai'i County is one of the country's most dangerous counties in which to live when my husband was researching insurance companies to cover our condo association. Here's what the Big Island has to deal with:

Hurricanes and Tropical Storms

While we have been here over the past eight years, we have had two Hurricane Flossie "near misses." They named them both Flossie, the first time in August 2007 and then again in August 2013.

The islands get an average of 4.5 tropical cyclones a year and one hurricane about every fifteen years. Last year, the central Pacific had five tropical cyclones after the National Oceanic and Atmospheric Administration predicted two to three.[1]

Iselle, the last hurricane to hit the island, caused millions of dollars in damage in the Eastern Puna district in August of 2014. Prior to Iselle, Iniki hit in 1992, ravaging Kauai, killing six people, and causing $2.5 billion in damage. Iniki raked the Big Island on its way through as well, causing coastal damage.

We even have a local weather phenomenon called "Kona Storms," a seasonal cyclone the island experiences each winter with heavy surf, high winds, and rain.

http://bit.ly/KonaStorms

Earthquakes

On October 15, 2006, Kailua-Kona was hit with a 6.7 magnitude earthquake. The earthquake caused property damage, injuries, landslides, power outages, and airport delays and closures. At least sixty-one buildings were destroyed. According to Wikipedia, "Almost all houses in West Hawai'i reported extensive internal damage, but most avoided significant structural damage, the reason being that most of the buildings in the area around the epicenter of the earthquake have been built in the last few decades and are well constructed. Even so, over $200 million in damage occurred."[2]

Tsunamis

On March 11, 2011, a 9.0 earthquake that hit Japan caused a destructive tsunami here in Kona, taking out several businesses in downtown Kona, and causing severe damage near our home in Keauhou. In fact, they are STILL repairing the damage caused at the Keauhou Pier area from when the Keauhou Kona Yacht Club building was raked by the continuous wave surge. Tens of millions of dollars in damage occurred around the Hawaiian Islands.

The most destructive tsunami in Hawai'i occurred on April 1, 1946, following an Aleutian Islands earthquake. Waves 55 feet high, crest to trough, struck the northeast coast of Hawai'i. In Hilo, 173 people were killed, 163 more were injured, 488 buildings were demolished, and 936 more were damaged. Damage was estimated at $25 million. The waterfront was washed out, and breakwater and wharves badly damaged.[3]

Volcanic Eruptions

Kilauea's current eruption dates back to January 3, 1983, and is by far its longest-lived historical period of activity, as well as one of the longest-lived eruptions in the world. According to Wikipedia, "As of January 2011, the eruption has produced 3.5 cubic kilometers (0.84 cubic miles) of lava and resurfaced 123.2 square kilometers (48 square miles) of land. Kilauea's entire known history has been an active volcano, and except for a brief pause between 1934 and 1952, has never experienced any prolonged period of rest." [4] Kilauea, the youngest of Hawai'i's volcanoes, is believed to be between 300,000 and 600,000 years of age. Ask anyone living on the east side of the island and they'll tell you that the volcano threat there is a real one, especially now, as the lava is advancing across the District of Puna towards the small town of Pahoa.

VOG — Volcanic Smog

When speaking of the fact that Kilauea (which means "spewing" in Hawaiian) has been going off for more than thirty years, you have to talk about what all the sulfur pouring out is doing to the air quality on the Big Island, and more specifically, to Kailua-Kona.

On Hawai'i Island, the gas plumes of Kilauea rise up from three locations: Halema'uma'u Crater, Pu'u 'Ō'ō vent, and from along the coastline, where lava flows from the East Rift zone[5] and enters the ocean. The plumes create a blanket of vog, which at times envelops the island. Vog mostly affects the Kona coast, where the prevailing trade winds blow it to the southwest, and southern winds then blow it north up the Kohala coast. Most mornings you can see the vog slowly creep across Hualalai and then dip into Kona.

On rare occasions, prolonged periods of southerly Kona winds can cause vog to affect the eastern side of the Island, as well as islands across the entire state. By the time the vog reaches other islands, the sulfur dioxide has largely dissipated, leaving behind ash, smoke, sulfates, and ammonia. To hear people in Oahu tell it, we are a source of constant pollution to them. The bad news is that some days you can't see the horizon on the ocean, or when you look across Kona, it looks like a grey, smoky day. People have developed breathing issues due to the vog. *West Today* released more information last fall in an article:
http://bit.ly/VogImpactsHealth

When the vog is blown out on days we call "High Def," everything is so bright and beautiful that we wish Pele would take a break for a few years.

Pele is on Our Side

When my husband and I were rushing to get water, batteries and such, and move our lanai furniture indoors when the first Hurricane Flossie was approaching, we wondered why some of our long-time neighbors were not battening down the hatches with us. Here's what a local resident said, "The way our volcanic mountains line up on our island causes major storms like hurricanes to dissipate. We know Pele is protecting us." The first time Flossie hit, in 2007, I thought they were crazy. But lo and behold, NOTHING hit us that time. Then when a Category 4 hurricane was bearing down on us in 2013, I still stocked up but watched the storm-tracking app we have on our iPhone. Just as they had said, the storm dropped to a tropical depression within one hundred miles of Hawai'i and we got a twenty-minute lashing.

Most recently, in August 2014, Hurricane Iselle came ashore near Ka'u on the Eastern side of the island. West Hawai'i barely saw any wind or rain, whereas coastal homes in Puna were destroyed, the power grid was debilitated for over two weeks, and hundreds of trees were blown over along the entire Eastern side of the island. Another hurricane following Iselle, Julio, was thankfully downgraded to a tropical depression and was sent glancing to the north of our island.

I'm not going to say that you shouldn't prepare for hurricanes— and after Iselle, many disaster aid professionals warned folks in West Hawai'i that they should not let their guard down—but I WILL say that if you believe in the power of Pele, or the geographic blessing of how our volcanoes (Mauna Loa, Hualalai, and Mauna Kea) are arranged, you can rest a little easier.

notes

1. Category 4 Hurricane Flossie keeps to its path toward ..,
http://www.wave3.com/story/6923573/category-4-hurricane-flossie-keeps-to-its-path-toward-hawaii-expected-to-weaken (accessed October 1, 2014).

2. 2006 earthquake - Wikipedia, the free encyclopedia,
http://en.wikipedia.org/wiki/2006_Hawaii_earthquake (accessed October 1, 2014).

3. - USGS Earthquake Hazard Program,
http://earthquake.usgs.gov/earthquakes/states/hawaii/history.php (accessed October 1, 2014).

4. Kīlauea - Wikipedia, the free encyclopedia, http://en.wikipedia.org/wiki/Kilauea (accessed October 1, 2014).

5. Vog: Bad Air from a Beautiful Volcano - Kauai Activities ..,
http://www.nanakai.com/see-kauai/vog-bad-air-from-a-beautiful-volcano.html (accessed October 1, 2014).

Chapter Three

Why Hawai'i is the Most Expensive Place to Live

So, you have decided to consider moving to Hawai'i because you want to wriggle your toes in the sand all year round, swim in a temperate ocean, sit under swaying palm trees, and eat non-GMO mangos and papayas. Right? Well, there is a price to pay for all this beauty, and the reasons are varied.

First, did you know that beyond the District of Columbia, Hawai'i is the most expensive state to live in America?
http://bit.ly/MostExpensivePlacesToLive

In August 2014, the Tax Foundation released a report using first-ever government data showing how the real value of $100 varies by state. As that map showed, a variety of factors conspire to make Hawai'i the state where $100 buys you the least ($85.32) and Mississippi the state where it can buy the most ($115.74).[1]

Most people think that Oahu and Maui are the most expensive islands, so they turn their attention to the Big Island for a more affordable alternative. Let me tell you, I thought the same thing when I bought a condo in Keauhou in 2005. Back then, condos were going for a million dollars in Oahu. What I did not factor in was the fact that there are more and better paying jobs on Oahu. Maui, too, has higher priced homes, but more tourists in a smaller space help to drive incomes up. On the Big Island, the average income in West Hawai'i is $50,000, but a three-bedroom house in a decent neighborhood is close to $600,000. You do the math. Real estate expenses are the leading driver of the high cost of living in Hawai'i.

Hawai'i Island has a long-term strategy for growth and it basically states that 70 percent of the land will be kept for farming, ranching, and open space, which includes massive lava fields. Economics would state that if you can't develop the land, the existing development becomes more expensive. I wrote a post about the reasons why many people don't live on this island, after I found people doing Google searches looking for this answer:

http://bit.ly/5ReasonsWhyPeopleDontLiveOnBigIsland

Currently, we are experiencing a rental-housing crunch that is not only making the cost of rents go up, but even finding a rental home is becoming more challenging. This usually causes people to consider BUYING a home, which, in turn, makes the cost of homes increase, a market force that is occurring in West Hawai'i right now. Be prepared to spend at least $1,200 a month for rent for a condo and upwards of $2,000 a month for a larger home. I post real estate statistics on my 365Kona blog and most local agents can provide you with real estate listings as they hit the market.

Let's talk about energy costs. Although Hawai'i has a long-term renewable energy plan in place, we are slow going in getting solar, wind, wave, and thermal power to take the place of our current diet of fossil fuels that need to be shipped to the island. I have spoken to many people considering a move to Kona, who ask me which subdivisions have air conditioning built into the homes. I ask if they plan on spending more than $200 on their electricity bill each month. If you want to be cooler when you move to Kona, find a home at the 1,000 or above elevation to get natural cooling, because fans and air conditioning will cost you A LOT. Personally, our condo down by the ocean runs a near constant eighty-seven degrees in the summer. We have learned to deal with the heat and take it easy on the fans. I know many tourists who come here and have to be in hotel rooms with air conditioning constantly running. If you want to live by the ocean, it is going to be warm. If you can't take the heat, you're going to pay for cool comfort.

Here are some sobering facts: Hawai'i is the only state that depends so heavily on petroleum for its energy needs.[2] Whereas less than 1 percent of electricity in the nation is generated using oil, Hawai'i relies on oil for 74 percent of its electricity generation. Here's a fantastic snapshot of Hawai'i's energy usage and charts showing where the energy is being used:

http://bit.ly/EnergyMapOfHawaii

The chart also points to another expensive monthly cost you'll need to survive here, and that's gasoline. When the rest of the country was crying over gas prices possibly hitting $4 a gallon, we had already hit the $4.50 a gallon mark. As I tell my friends, we arrived just as Hurricane Katrina was hitting New Orleans and the gas prices spiked around the country. Well, they never came back down in Kona. We switched from a minivan to a Scion to help with the monthly fuel costs. Some folks just expect to pay at the pump and still drive their big trucks around town, but it adds up for services that need to rely on transportation to deliver goods and services to the residents of the island.

People think that if they move here from California food costs should be about the same. "*Au contraire, mon frère*," as my mother used to say. Food costs are about 30 percent more than on the mainland because they need to be shipped over 2,500 miles if by boat, or flown here using expensive jet fuel. There's also the high cost of labor, land, and energy to get water to the crops for locally grown food. Top that off with grocers needing to keep more products on their shelves vs. their mainland counterparts because they are further away from the source.

I remember when, after living on the island for a year, we moved back to the Bay Area for a while. I walked into Trader Joes and almost wept at being able to buy a loaf of bread for $2.50. I wanted to kiss the floor in front of the dairy area while paying 60 cents for a container of

23

yogurt vs. $1.40 here in Kona. We are currently paying $7 for a loaf of whole grain bread and $18 a pound for freshly caught fish, which is not uncommon. Those fishermen have to use a lot of gas while trolling for fish in our waters. Energy costs affect everything.

The point that needs to be made here, especially if you are starting a business, and yet another factor that affects the cost of living: taxes. We have a pyramid of taxes that rolls down to each person who *touches* a service or product. 4 percent does not seem like much, but it's charged for everything, and if it goes from producer to middle man to consumer, it can end up being 12 percent. In California, they don't tax food. Nothing escapes taxes in Hawai'i.

I tell you this not to scare you away from living here. What I want to do is prepare you for other costs you will have to work into your monthly budget. Some of you have told me you are coming with a sizable nest egg to start your new life in Hawai'i. That's fantastic if that's the case, but a friend of mine who lived here for one year on his retirement got his teaching credentials and is now a substitute teacher at the local junior high school. He made that choice when he saw how fast his retirement savings were going. Those eleven-dollar hamburgers and nine-dollar Mai Tais, along with your rent, grocery, electricity, gas, and entertainment costs can definitely change your idea of lounging on a beach chair all day. At least in most of the cases I see . . . and again, if you are fortunate enough to live in Kukio and have a butler delivering your Pina Coladas to your poolside chair, you didn't need to read this chapter!

notes

1. Map: How much $100 is really worth in hundreds of ..,
http://www.washingtonpost.com/blogs/govbeat/wp/2014/08/20/map-how-much-100-is-really-worth-in-hundreds-of-metropolitan-areas (accessed October 7, 2014).

2. Facility Input (feedstocks) Output (products) Production Capacity,
http://energy.hawaii.gov/wp-content/uploads/2011/08/HI-Energy-FactsFigures_May2014_2r.pdf (accessed October 7, 2014).

Chapter Four

Most Desirable Places to Live in West Hawai'i

Through my blogging, I see many people asking and searching for an answer to the question: "Where is the best place to live on the Big Island of Hawai'i?" Having lived here for four years straight, and four years before that coming on and off the island as a part-time resident, I have three answers.

1. If you have a lot of money, the best place to live is in Hualalai. That's where the Four Seasons Resort is located, along with million dollar homes and a few billionaire neighbors. They are in the rain shadow of Hualalai, so they really avoid almost all types of inclement weather, including wind. You will also find Kukio, another adjacent uber-rich neighborhood. See aerial shot of this area and you'll see why.

2. Keauhou, where I live, ROCKS! I met a couple who were considering buying the condo next door to us, and they were on the fence about buying it before they met me. After a few beers in the kitchen, and telling them all the great reasons why Keauhou was the place to be in Hawai'i, they put an offer on the condo that night. THAT'S how much I love living here! It's a little upscale, so we have NO crime! The area is situated around a golf course, right near Keauhou Bay, with all types of ocean activities and within a mile of the grocery store, a movie theater, restaurants, a Longs Drug Store, Sam Choy's Kai Lanai, the Kona Sheraton, and one of the best snorkeling bays in the whole Hawaiian Island chain. It's basically a sub-division and there are no schools here, so it's not the perfect place for children, as mostly retirees and condo investors buy here. The condo next to us sold for about $245,000, which gives you an idea of the cost for a one-bed/one bath-

condo here. The area above where I live, Keauhou Estates, is gated and has beautiful large homes for between $600,000 and $1,000,000.

3. If you are a working stiff, coming to the island not to retire but to live here full-time, there are some neighborhoods that are fantastic above Lako Street, especially in the Sunset area. South Kona has the most affordable housing for average families, which includes many of my friends. They get a fair amount of rain there, so I'd say if you want the best weather and a great view, Holualoa is a quaint farm/artist community at about 1,500 feet, so it's at least ten degrees cooler than down by the water, which is where I am in Keauhou. They also have a VERY good school and you can shoot right down the road to the ocean. Those are, in my humble opinion, the best places to live on the Big Island.

Other Options

For those who love rain and relatively little vog, Hilo is a *real* town with more job opportunities than Kona. Did I say they get a lot of rain?

Waimea is upcountry and has its fair share of misty, rainy weather on the side coming in from Hilo, and a VERY dry side coming towards Kohala. This is *Paniolo* (Hawaiian Cowboy) country, so you'll see plenty of horses and you'll even get to attend an occasional rodeo! Lots of people who live there have been there for generations. If I moved to a tropical island, I would want to be warm and near the water . . . just sayin'.

Waimea does have two of the best private schools on the island, if that's a priority to you. And it's close to most of the major resorts along the Kohala Coast.

Hawi and North Kohala have very few of what I would call "creature comforts." There's no theater, shopping center, ocean side dining, etc. BUT, many tech titans have found a little piece of farming paradise there, and many who live in this northernmost and very quaint part of the island would live nowhere else on Earth. They simply love it.

Waikoloa and Waikoloa Village have their issues of being out in the middle of a lava flow with a LOT of wind, as that area sits in a wind tunnel created by the two volcanoes, Mauna Kea and Mauna Loa. They do not receive much rain there, but the wind! Oy! Waikoloa Village was built as the "workforce housing" for the resorts along the Kohala coast. Waikoloa Village is a family oriented place with good schools, close proximity to the resorts, and has reasonably priced real estate. Locally famous chef, James Babian, opened a restaurant there called Pueo's Osteria and it's the best Italian restaurant on the island. Waikoloa has quite a few luxury condos, which are good investment opportunities for vacation rentals. This area also has the upscale Queens MarketPlace and King's Shops, which, along with the resorts, provide job opportunities for residents.

The Kona-Kohala Chamber of Commerce has a great relocation package if you are really thinking of moving here, and like I said, the Realtors in Kona are very helpful resources for information about moving to and living on this island.

Chapter Five

Why You Can't Decide Where to Buy Until You Live Here

Before moving to Kona, many of you have probably driven around and thought about where would you live if you could be here full time. Some of you may be thinking that you know Kona well enough, that if a great home were for sale you could make an offer after a short visit, and you probably could. However, just about everyone who has lived here for any length of time will tell you that you have to spend months here to really learn about the neighborhoods, microclimates, vog patterns, etc., in order to find what will truly be the best fit for YOU.

Neighborhoods

Kona has a variety of neighborhoods, subdivisions, and farms, all within a ten-mile area. Where you want your children to attend school, and where you want to walk to a park, run your dog, walk to a beach, not sit in morning traffic, get downtown easily, be out of a high density housing area, run down Ali'i Drive, etc. will determine where you want to look for a home. Your lifestyle will dictate the neighborhood you want to live in, and you won't get a lifestyle until you get your groove on here!

Elevation

I get people asking questions like this on my blog: "I want to live near the ocean. Which condo complexes have air conditioning?" Remember when we spoke about energy costs? Running air conditioning in Kona will cost, depending upon the square footage of the home, between $200 and $400 a month. You can use that money to rent or buy a home at the 1,000-foot elevation, using only fans, with the cool mountain air breezing through your home. We live at seventy-five feet above ocean level and have learned to live with eighty-eight degree indoor air temps during the summer. The first year you live here, you will probably spend time acclimating to the humidity and weather. Why do you think all the most desirable homes for full-time residents are at the 1,000 to 2,000-foot elevation? However, what you sacrifice for cool air, you miss in not being able to easily get to the beach. My *mountain* friends who live at the 2,500 to 3,000-foot elevation LOVE the cool air, but they deal with moisture issues and have to constantly run dehumidifiers to stop their clothing, bedding, etc. from mildewing. Personally, we have run the gamut of deciding the cloud forest was the place for us at 3,000 feet, to wanting to live on a coffee farm at 1,500 feet, to living in the Pualani subdivision at 1,000 feet, to staying put so we could run to the Sheraton for our coffee several days a week.

Mauka/Makai Trade winds

Did you know that Mark Twain spent time in Kona, and in 1866 wrote about his experiences for *The Sacramento Union* in correspondences that have come to be known as "Letters From Hawaii"? I read one of these letters where he wrote about the tropical trade winds coming down from Hualalai in the morning and then back up again in the afternoon. He used beautiful words of floating, scented plumeria breezes, and rustling palm fronds. These trade winds, or "trades" as we refer to them, run *mauka/makai* from the mountain to the ocean. When the Hawaiians built their homes, they made sure to situate their homes to take advantage of Mother Nature's natural cooling effect. You will find that there are homes in Kona that were not designed to capture the trades.

I recently met a woman who stood on an open cement pad in Pulalani Estates, bought the land, and came back to the island after they built the house. They built her master bedroom in a manner that stopped all airflow from coming into the home, and she ended up having to install air conditioning. My friend who lives directly below her sits on her lanai enjoying her ocean views, with the trades blowing in her hair every afternoon, and never even turns on her fans. It makes a

HUGE difference. Before you buy or rent, see what the trades do. When we first came to the island, we rented a small ocean-level condo tucked into the middle of the complex with no air flow and I cried every day when it was ninety degrees in there. I had to stick my ten-month-old baby's head into the freezer with two air conditioning units blaring. You think I'm kidding?

Cost of Housing

Do you want to live in Kona? There are homes that are a lot less expensive in smaller communities all over the island. I am not going to say anything negative about any of the outlying towns or anything on the east side of the island, but what I WILL say is this: If you think you are going to buy a home for less than $300,000, you will be dealing with many quality of life issues, not the least of which are long commutes, crime, drugs, coqui frogs, lack of job opportunities, isolation, and the worst part, spotty Wi-Fi!

Using a Realtor as a Tour Guide

I will speak on behalf of my Realtor friends on this one. Gas is expensive here. Time is money and Realtors are not tour guides. If you want to get the lay of the land, get a rental car and start looking around. You will know if you want to learn more about a neighborhood just by seeing it. I found out pretty quickly that I did not want to see homes located in the areas where mattresses were on the front lawns, or where I could hear the garbage trucks coming every morning at the crack of dawn in a high-density housing area. Drive around at different times of the day in the neighborhoods you think you might want to live in, THEN call a Realtor to ask about the homes available in those areas. If you are not sure if you want to live in Honoka'a, Kohala, or Hilo, avoid asking a Realtor to drive you for miles to help you decide.

Feel the Energy

When you move to Hawai'i, let's face it, you are going to see for yourself that there is an energy to living here that you don't find anywhere else. Each part of the island has a different energy and people resonate individually with that energy.

Kealekekua Bay and that area attracts healers, Keauhou Bay has a high vibrational frequency, and the energy you get from being in the cloud forest off of Koloko Road is very peaceful. You have to really FEEL the energy around the area you want to call home. Some folks are more sensitive to energies than others. We brought in spiritual guides to bless our condo with a traditional Hawaiian ceremony to clear any negative energy and promote peace and tranquility. When people visit us, they say they can feel the peacefulness in our home.

When anyone breaks ground on a building project in Hawai'i, a *Kahu* performs a traditional Hawaiian blessing. *Kahu* is a Hawaiian word that literally means caretaker. *Kahu* (or *Kahuna*, which is a respected leader and advisor), is derived from the concept of being the caretaker of the culture, and is usually an elder in society.

When I first arrived in Hawai'i I did not know, understand, or believe in a lot of the spiritual/energetic traditions here. Now? Let me say this: if you believe in it or not, it's still there.

If you would like a traditional Hawaiian blessing of your home, ask your Realtor, or you can call the Ecumenical Church of Light and they can help you.

Chapter Six

Getting Zen About Your Stuff: Things to Leave Home And Why

As we discussed previously, shipping to Hawai'i is expensive. You just can't take it all with you and you'll find that you won't want to either.

Did you read my "58 Boxes" story?
http://bit.ly/58BoxesLeavingMyStuffBehind

In that blog post, I detail my painful experience of selling, giving away, and throwing away my "stuff" in order to live in my Kona condo. There's a whole spiritual/deep soul cleaning aspect when you have to look at everything you own and decide what to ship, store, and/or give away. Many of my readers reached out to me after I wrote that blog post to let me know about their own painful, yet rewarding experience in cutting the clutter and becoming less burdened by stuff.

I have seen the other extreme as well—people spending thousands of dollars putting their entire home and life into Matson shipping containers. There is not ONE person I have met who EVER said they did the right thing by moving it all over here. Why?

Why You Should Not Ship Your Old Life to Kona

1. You just don't need your family's antiques, nor do you need every stick of furniture. For the antiques, they'll get ruined with the humidity, or the mold if you live at a higher elevation, and since space is at a premium here that type of furniture is just not practical. I recently dealt with this myself when my mom passed away and I wanted to ship her mahogany table and

chairs to Kona. My husband had to keep reminding me of how expensive it would be to ship them and how they may not hold up for the long haul near the ocean.

There are a few exceptions. If you have an exceptional sofa bed, bring it for your guests who will visit. We spent over $2,000 on ours, which was a great deal looking back, nine years later. Really good sofa beds are hard to come by and they're expensive. There are a lot of garage sales from people moving off the island, and I have seen a few used ones at the Habitat for Humanity REStore near Costco. The ebb and flow of residents keeps the used furniture market going.

2. You will never have a chance to wear everything that is currently hanging in your closet or sitting in your drawers and under-bed carrier. You don't need much over here. Shorts, a few swimsuits, tank tops/t-shirts, some sundresses, etc. Men will find that Aloha shirts will get them invited into a conversation a lot faster than swanky modern wear from Diesel. Nightlife here in Kona does not warrant your five-inch heels, unless you are twenty-two. As I mentioned before, you are coming here to live a simpler lifestyle, right? Designer suits, ties, blouses, pumps, loafers, dress jackets, etc. are just not needed. You'll find yourself looking at photos of yourself in a few years wearing the same tank tops, floral blouses, and Tommy Bahama shirts. If you DO plan on living at a high elevation, go ahead and bring the sweaters, scarves, blankets, and sweatshirts. You should bring a few jackets anyway for your trips to Volcano, Waimea, and Mauna Kea. It will take you a while to realize you don't need a light jacket, sweater, or shawl to go out in the evening around the ocean. If you DO find yourself a bit chilly, it will be in the over-air conditioned resort ballrooms, movie theaters, restaurants, and places that can afford the energy costs to keep

large spaces cooled! I only wear my jeans and a sweater when I go to see movies at the Keauhou Theaters.

3. Once you get it all over here, you find it does not quite fit where you need it. Then you have to store it. Then you have to pay for storage. Then it continues to be a drag on your new life.

4. Think about getting a Kindle before shipping all your novels and books over here.

A friend I met through my 365 Kona blog, John, offers this advice:

"The best advice I had was not to ship household goods such as furniture. I have found that what you have on the mainland just doesn't work here. Save the expense and sell everything, except memorabilia. Ship what you can USPS parcel post. It takes a few weeks, but is much cheaper. Come find a turnkey place to live in while you're looking for something long term. Do that a few MONTHS in advance. Unless you love your car, or it's paid for, think about getting something here. Having a 4X4 to enjoy some of the hard-to-get-to places is fantastic, so definitely bring your truck if you have one. We make a lot of trips to Lowe's and Home Depot. Good luck! I planned way ahead of time and my move was very successful!"

Shipping Your Car

I would suggest you leave vehicles on the mainland that don't have access to a Hawai'i Island dealership. Getting replacement parts is not only expensive, it may take days or WEEKS to get the part on the island. You will find this to be true of many things, which will leave you frustrated that you live on an island 2,500 miles from anywhere, but you will learn to plan for it.

Toyotas are the number one vehicle on the island and since there are so many, the parts are relatively affordable and available. Honda also has a large presence here. We have a BMW dealership, along with Ford, Mazda, and Hyundai. Just do a Google search for your car make and find out what's available in West Hawai'i.

My hubby, who is a "car guy," has this to say:

"The island's humidity and salty air wreak havoc on electrical systems in cars. You may wish to pick a car that you don't mind growing old quicker than you think."

Rust is rampant, along with fading paint, and just about everyone gets "lava bites" in their bumpers from backing into short lava walls. Another thing to remember is that some vehicles need special order tires, which means you can't expect to just show up at Costco and have your tires replaced.

When you come over, you will need to have a vehicle safety inspection before they will give you your vehicle registration. They will ensure everything is in working condition on your car, like no cracks in the windshield, lights working, seatbelts in place, etc. You can get the safety checks done at local garages, like Lex Brodie's.

We have plenty of used vehicles and Craigslist is always hopping with people who are making the transition off the island, too.

Shipping Companies

Matson is the shipping company most people use.
http://bit.ly/MatsonShipping

DHX is used by quite a few local companies.
http://bit.ly/DependableHawaiianExpress-DHX

UPS gets things here faster than if it goes by "boat," as we say.
http://bit.ly/UPSHawaii

To give you an idea of the price to ship items here, take a look at this site that gives you competitive pricing against USPS.
http://bit.ly/ShippingPriceComparison

When you see the expense of shipping your items over here, or if you have to store it, you begin to see why people have blowout garage sales before they move here. You can cry over your stuff in your driveway, like I did, or over the shipping and storage bills.

Because we live twenty-five hundred miles away from the mainland, *overnighting* anything from the mainland takes two days, whether it's via USPS, FedEx, or UPS. This is true especially if it's coming from east of the Mississippi.

Chapter Seven

Moving Your Precious Pet to Kona: The Good, the Bad, and the Ugly

When people with pets think about living the good life in Hawai'i, invariably they turn to their pets and think about quarantine requirements. As you may know, Hawai'i does not have rabies and they have worked hard to make sure it stays that way.

In order to ensure this, they used to make pet owners jump through a variety of hoops to get pets to the island. You still need to have your pet start the process of getting shots and going through quarantine at least 120 days before coming to Hawai'i, but they can be in quarantine in your home instead of a quarantine center on the island. You should look into the costs of vet bills for shots, transport, quarantine, etc. to get an idea of how expensive it may be to bring your pet with you. Here is the definitive information from the State of Hawai'i Animal Industry Division.
http://bit.ly/FAQForAnimalQuarantine

The Good
Many people move their pets to Hawai'i successfully and the pets live out a very happy existence here. Once you get past the trip to the island, make sure you get them licensed and chipped. You may also wish to find a local vet before you need one.

We like the **Keauhou Vet** as they are up the street from us.
http://bit.ly/KeauhouVet

My friends also like **Ali'i Veterinary Hospital.**
http://bit.ly/AliiVet

To help your pet travel safely, comfortably, and in style, check out this site that offers pet airline travel supplies.

http://bit.ly/DryFur

If you want some help locally, **A Kona Pet** is a pet relocation service.

http://bit.ly/AKonaPetRelocation

Island Pet Movers

http://bit.ly/IslandPetMovers

Happy Tails Travel

http://bit.ly/HappyTailsPetMoving

The Bad

Size and Breed Restrictions for Flying Your Pet

Check with the airlines about size and breed restrictions. As my friend says, "Especially the bully breeds. This pertains to pugs, pit bulls, terriers, bulldogs, and any breed with a short nose. Some airlines won't even fly certain breeds. There is also a size issue. Many airlines, including Hawaiian, will only take dogs up to a certain weight. For instance, they would not have accepted flying my 120-pound Rottweiler because she was too big. Some airlines refuse to fly certain dogs because of outdated notions of dangerous breeds."

Lack of Dog-Friendly Parks and Beaches

If you had envisioned taking long walks on the beach with your un-leashed dog, you'll want to pay attention here. Hawai'i County can be very unfriendly when it comes to pets. A friend of mine who has lived here for twenty years, owns four dogs, and is involved in island pet events and groups says, "Living on Maui, I was accustomed to taking my dog to the beach every weekend. Here, on the Big Island, dogs are banned from EVERY County park and beach. People should be aware of the rules. There are a few places that dogs are allowed, but many are word of mouth. For me, NOT being able to take my dog to the local beach is a BIG deal and was part of the reason it took me a long time to adjust to the Big Island." There IS a beach the locals call "Dog Beach" near the Honokohau Harbor, which allows dogs to run free, but you have to scramble over rocks to get there. Here's a video showing you what it takes to get there:

http://bit.ly/HonokohauDogBeach

All state campgrounds will not allow you to bring your pets, so if camping is your hobby, you will have to find areas that are off the beaten path.

The Ugly

If your animal is like your child, you may wish to check the airline's record for animal deaths, injury, and loss. Here's the May 2014 report for all major domestic airlines:

http://bit.ly/AnimalAirlineIncidentReports

Also, consider the time of year you intend to bring your pet over. Summer may not be a good time if you live in a hot environment. Call either of the vets listed above for more tips and information, and to make sure you have all the facts about moving your pet to Hawai'i.

Point to note

We had friends move to Hawai'i in February and they brought a small dog and a cat. Finding a rental home with two animals hampered their ability to find housing quickly. As of the time of this guide's publishing, Kona is experiencing a rental housing shortage and pets are a liability. The only hotel that allows pets is the Fairmont Orchid at $300 a night. Our friends had to kennel their animals at $25 each, per day. If you are coming to rent a home, and you have pets, you will want to secure housing before you arrive. Trust me.

Chapter Eight

Resource Guide to Make Moving Easier and Getting Set Up

This resource guide is your Golden Ticket to getting set up as you begin your move.

Moving Your Stuff

We talked about not bringing everything with you, but if you DO find yourself needing more than a few duffle bags, here are some moving service companies that can help:

Kona Trans
(808) 329-4111
http://www.konatrans.com

Royal Hawaiian Movers
1-888-717-6925
http://bit.ly/RoyalHawaiianMovers

Moving Your Car

Here are a few local resources to consider for shipping your car to Hawai'i. Remember, you have to ship your car with nothing in it. I know when I first thought of shipping our minivan over to Kona, I assumed I could fill it with all my boxes. Nope. They may let you leave a car seat in there if you're lucky.

Matson
1-800-4MATSON
http://bit.ly/MatsonShipping

Hawaii Car Transport
(808) 445-6695
http://bit.ly/ShipACarToHawaii

Getting Your Electricity Turned On

HELCO (Hawaiian Electric Light Company) is the main electric company. They suggest giving them at least a two-day heads up to get your power turned on. A service establishment charge of twenty dollars is required to start or reconnect electric service. There is an additional charge of twenty-five dollars for same-day service requests.
(808) 548-7311
http://bit.ly/HawaiiElectricLight

Getting Your Water Turned On

Department of Water Supply, County of Hawai'i. To get your water service turned on or prevent it from being turned off, you will need to give them a one hundred dollar security deposit.
(808) 322-0600
http://bit.ly/HawaiiDepartmentOfWater

Getting Your Cable/DSL

Oceanic Time Warner Cable is a service provider for TV, Internet, Home Phone, and Home Security. Remember to allow at least a week, sometimes two, for the cable guys to show up and connect you.
(808) 643-2100
http://bit.ly/OceanicTimeWarner

Free Wi-Fi

If you find yourself without Wi-Fi when you move here, you can go downtown while waiting for Oceanic to get you set up and get free Wi-Fi at Java on the Rock from *6 a.m. to 10 a.m.*, and at Daylight Mind Coffee Company and Starbucks all day long, seven days a week. There is also the Kona Library, which has computers for public use.

Getting Your Telephone Land Line

Hawaiian Telecom
Offers bundles for phone and TV
1-877-482-2211
http://bit.ly/HawaiiTelComm

Mobile Phone

Both your Verizon and ATT services should work fine here in Kona. Sprint customers say they get frequent dropped calls.

Here is the link for Verizon that also offers home bundles of services.
http://bit.ly/VerizonInternetTVPhone

Getting Your Driver's License

Department of Motor Vehicles
(808) 323-4800
West Hawai'i Civic Center, 75-5044 Ane Keohokalole Highway (near the harbor)

Stop by Longs Drugstore and pick up the Driver's License Manual to take the test. You can also go to the DMV site to take practice tests online:
http://bit.ly/HawaiiMotorVehicleOffice

You will need some form of proof of license eligibility from the last state in which you held a license, and you'll need to take a driving test.

Heads up

For married women, bring your birth certificate and marriage license. They make you jump through some extra hoops if you've changed your name. The wait can be long, so get there right when they open.

Registering your vehicle

Motor Vehicle Registration
(808) 323-4818
While you are at the DMV, register your vehicle too. You will also need to have a vehicle safety inspection before they will finalize the registration of your vehicle. You can download the forms you will need from here:
http://bit.ly/DownloadableFormsHawaii

Bank Account

There are no mainland *mega* banks here in Hawai'i. Here's a list of some of the more popular financial institutions:

Bank of Hawai'i
(808) 326-3900
https://www.boh.com

First Hawaiian Bank
1-888-844-4444
http://bit.ly/FirstHawaiianBank

Central Pacific Bank
(808) 935-5251
http://www.centralpacificbank.com

American Savings Bank
(808) 329-5281
http://www.asbhawaii.com

Hawai'i Community Federal Credit Union
(808) 930-7700
http://www.hicommfcu.com

HFS Federal Credit Union
(808) 322-2121
http://www.hfsfcu.org

Make sure you know your rental rights before signing a lease agreement. You are moving to a new state. Each state has different rules and regs for landlord/tenants rights. It's a good idea to familiarize yourself with the information before signing an agreement.
http://bit.ly/LandlordTenantInformation

Health Care

General Care Practitioner
Based upon the health insurance you get here, you should check to see what your insurance provider has in their care provider section, and call and see if they are taking new patients. It's always a good idea to make an appointment with a doctor and say Aloha BEFORE you need one.

Pediatricians In Kona
Many pediatricians are not taking new patients. Call ahead of time to see if your insurance carrier is accepted and if the doctor is taking on

new patients, especially if you are bringing young children who need regular physicals.

http://bit.ly/KonaPediatricians

Getting Your Child a TB Test

Before you can enroll your children in school, you will need to get them a TB test. You can do this at the County Health Services or through your child's own doctor. Here are the locations, times, and phone numbers of the County Health Clinics.

http://bit.ly/ClinicSchedule

Health Care Centers

Major West Hawai'i hospitals are located in Kealakekua and Waimea. There is an Urgent Care in Keauhou Shopping Center, which is highly recommended for emergencies. They are open *9 a.m. to 9 p.m.*, seven days a week, and can be a good alternative to the hospital emergency room.

Kona Community Hospital (808) 322-9311

North Hawai'i Community Hospital (808) 885-4444

Kaiser Permanente Medical Center Outpatient Clinic
    (808) 432-3400

Straub Clinic and Family Health Care Center (808) 329-9744

Keauhou Urgent Care Center (808) 322-2544

Kona Urgent Care Center (808) 327-4357

American Cancer Society, West Hawai'i Unit (808) 334-0442

Veterans Services (808) 969-3833

Big Island HIV/Aids Foundation (808) 322-1718

Alternative Health Providers

The list of alternative healers on the West Side of Hawai'i is lengthy, so I have only included a few here. There is just about every type of healing modality represented in Hawai'i, including acupuncture, chiropractic, massage therapy, Lomi Lomi, aromatherapy, etc. We even had a healer who was able to ask my husband's spirit guides to tell her what was wrong with him, and the best cure for him!

Kona Family Health Center
(808) 329-9211
http://bit.ly/KonaFamilyHealth

Kona Wellness Center for Integrative Medicine
Dr. Denisa Maruyama and Dr. Ty Vincent MD
(808) 331-8404
http://konawellness.com

Michael Traub, ND (Naturopathic Doctor)
(808) 329-2114
http://bit.ly/MichaelTraubND

Ilona Honig (Hawaiian healer and massage therapist)
(808) 658-0326
IDreamBeach@aol.com

Dentists in Kona
You can do a Google search for dentists in Kona, but I will give you two top-notch professionals that our family has personally used:

Dr. Gabriel Uy, DDS
(808) 329-8899

Dr. Melissa Beaudet-Uy
(808) 329-7351

Tips on Living in Kona Successfully

Chapter Nine

Get Active, Get Involved, Have Fun

My family and I moved to Kona on a hot August day, almost ten years ago, not knowing a soul beyond our Realtor. We had a ten-month-old baby and a three-year-old, and no idea what resources were available to help us meet new friends. For the first few weeks I was very lonely and began to regret the decision, having lived in my hometown for thirty years. But then I got involved with my oldest child's school's fundraising events, found a great church, started meeting people while running, and the next thing I knew I was involved in an active community!

When I hear my single friends who come to the island say they cry themselves to sleep at night, I know that loneliness can be a difficult issue here. Being out in the middle of the Pacific Ocean on an island is ISOLATING. There are other people who choose the Big Island to call home, thinking that the isolation is one of the best features. Those folks can skip this chapter!

We are very far away from some of the issues that seem to plague the mainland, and many people feel that if things were to fall apart in this world, we would be in a pretty good place to survive. (Although we do suffer from a food security issue due to our heavy reliance on those boats that keep showing up with supplies . . . but that's another topic.)

People come here sometimes to "get away from it all," and that's exactly what they get most days. However, spiritually, you never get away from yourself, and your problems have a way of following you here. The island has a pretty intense energy that has a way of really making you look at yourself. I'm just letting you know that coming here WILL change your life, and you get to choose how that's going to look for you. If you don't make an effort to get out and meet people in a variety of avenues, with an open attitude, you may be lonely.

Here are a few ways to avoid that feeling and find a sense of community in Kona:

Find and Join a Church or Synagogue

The first thing we did was find a church. Although we were not extremely religious per se, we knew it was our best hope in a new town to make friends. We sampled a few churches and found a nice Ohana in a small spiritual congregation near Koloko. From this group we found friendship, a few job opportunities, a place to come to for the holidays, and the added bonus—a group of healers and therapists in the mix that we've utilized numerous times over the years. *West Hawai'i Today* has an entire page of West Hawai'i churches, meetings, temples, etc. to choose from. My friend Beth, who is Jewish, says there are no synagogues on the island, but there is an active congregation, Kona Beth Shalom, that now has a home in the Kings Shops at the Mauna Lani:
> http://bit.ly/KonaBethShalom

Here is a helpful link with contact information for places of worship around the Big Island.
> http://bit.ly/KonaChurchDirectory

Some people find spirit in other places beyond a church. You can join the various canoe clubs in Kona to meet some amazing people who feel connected to the ocean, the sport, the culture, and the Ohana of the paddlers. There are two local clubs:

Kai 'Opua Canoe Club, one of the oldest canoe clubs in the state of Hawai'i, practices from downtown Kona.
> https://www.kaiopua.org

Keauhou Canoe Club, which has the strongest recreational paddling club in the state, practices from Keauhou Bay.

http://www.keauhoucanoeclub.com

Volunteer

There is MUCH to be done in Kona! Volunteer opportunities exist in many facets of life here and most can be researched on the web, including KonaWeb.com, and in the newspaper, *West Hawai'i Today*. My retired friend, Leah, serves meals to the homeless downtown on Mondays, and my husband is the President of the school board at my children's school. We always need help for the Big Island Chocolate Festival, the IronMan Foundation needs help for the race, and the Humane Society needs help at the shelter and with their fundraising activities, etc. You can volunteer at the Aloha Theater for their performances, or the Kahilu Theatre in Waimea, take part in a beach clean up with the World WildLife Fund, and donate your talent at the Donkey Mill Art Center for their Arts activities. You can build more bike trails with PATH, and lend your engineering and computer talent to students through the STEM programs. Volunteering will immerse you into the giving culture of Hawai'i; you'll make new friends and get a sense of community.

Go to Events

There are events almost every weekend in Kona or somewhere else on the Big Island. This includes free cultural events, fundraising races, arts and theater performances, festivals, and *hoolaulea* events, which is Hawaiian for "celebration." You can find an events calendar at KonaWeb.com, and I am working with a group of artists to keep a pretty comprehensive list going on the "Hawai'i Arts and Entertainment" Facebook page. The Hawaiian Tourism Authority has a great Events and Festivals page on their Big Island of Hawai'i page:

http://bit.ly/GoHawaiiEventsPage

For live theater performances, check the Aloha Performing Arts Theater site.
> http://www.apachawaii.org

And the Kahilu Theater in Waimea brings in top talent from around the world.
> http://kahilutheatre.org/Home

Train for a race

If you like running, go into the Big Island Running Company in downtown Kona and ask them about their running team. They have organized training runs weekly, which culminate in races such as the Peaman or the Team Mango races.

Peaman Races are FREE and you can get the kids involved, too!
> http://BigIslandRaces.com

Team Mango races are also free and you join the club by volunteering. This is a great option if you want to start training for a triathlon. Check out their site:
> http://teammangoraces.com

Join a Service Club

We have very active chapters for the Elks and Lions Clubs. If you are a resident under the age of forty, the Lions have a "young group" that is very social. My friend John is a member of the Elks and enjoys their weekly dancing night and dinner socials.
> Lions: http://bit.ly/LionsClubOfKona
> Elks: http://bit.ly/KonaElksClub

Join a Business Club

Getting to know the members of the local business community, if you are not retired, is paramount for financial success in Kona. Building relationships and connecting with the business community is key in getting people to trust you and start your referrals to build your business. Personally, I am a member of the Kona Kohala Chamber of Commerce, and I volunteer on the marketing committee. I also attended quite a few BNI (Business Network International) meetings and found them to be fun and young at heart, with driven professionals. A lawyer friend of mine who recently moved here joined the Rotary Club and almost immediately got several great business leads.

Kona Kohala Chamber of Commerce
http://www.kona-kohala.com

Kona Rotary Club
http://www.rotaryclubofkona.com

Kona Krew of BNI (BNI has two chapters in Kona, one meets in the morning and the other in the afternoon.)
http://www.bnikonakrew.com

Join "Mommy and Me" Groups
There is a Meetup group that works to put together events and activities for young children and their moms.
http://www.meetup.com/KonaMoms

If you drive down Ali'i Drive on Sundays, you can't help but see the jumpy houses and other activities for children at Living Stones Church. Many families enjoy that church for their camp and kid-friendly activities.
http://livingstones.us

Playgrounds

If you have toddlers, you'll find other moms at one of Kona's three playgrounds.

Higashihara Park on the way to South Kona:
http://bit.ly/HigashiharaPark

The newly renovated Kailua Playground near downtown:
http://bit.ly/KailuaPlayground

Pualani Park (The Blue Park) off of Queen K:
http://bit.ly/PualaniBluePark

Join a Meetup Group for Singles and People Looking for Fun

Kona Socials exists to provide fun and innovative activities that support all areas of life, including social, physical, mental, and spiritual **ones,** while allowing members of the community to connect and make empowering and meaningful friendships.
http://bit.ly/MeetupKonaOptimists

These groups and ideas are not complete, but they give you a taste of what is available here. I love my Kona community for all the fun and varied things to do, and the incredible people who reside here. I hope you will get involved and enjoy a true sense of community in Kona.

Chapter Ten

Connect Before You Arrive: Use Social Media and Online Resources

If you just read, in Chapter Nine, about all the cool clubs, churches, teams, organizations, and Meetup groups you can belong to in Kona, then know that you can start getting involved with them BEFORE you get here!

Do some online research using the links I provided, and connect with the organizers and leaders of the groups. Let them know when you are coming and set up some "meet and greet" time with them. You'll find a sense of Aloha among the folks who want to welcome you to your new island home.

A new friend of mine, Colin Jevins, whom I met on his exploratory trip to Kona to buy a coffee farm, knew me from my 365Kona blog on Facebook. He started finding and following people he felt were the "movers and shakers" in Kona, and then made it point to reach out and meet in person with many of them while he was visiting. He is going to have a host of new friends when he shows up here! Use social networking to make connections. There are quite a few of us on Twitter and Instagram, just search the hashtag #Kona.

You can also get a feeling for the community by liking, reading, and asking questions on Kona Facebook business pages. I have met some amazing people through social media that have helped me find job opportunities, as well as resource information for my blog and events I implement and promote.

Many connected and interesting people are posting on Pinterest and YouTube, too. You can do a search for images on Pinterest or videos on YouTube in Kona and West Hawai'i and meet some great local photographers, videographers, crafters, small business owners, and more.

Another way to reach out prior to coming to the island is contacting the Kona-Kohala Chamber of Commerce and asking them to send you a relocation package. They have a beautiful magazine with in-depth information, including Kona business listings with email addresses. I have mentioned quite a few times that showing up without a job or a clear way of making a living is NOT a good idea. By reaching out to the business community using this Resource Guide, you have the contact information for many of West Hawai'i's largest employers.

http://bit.ly/RelocationPacket

Chapter Eleven

Making a Living in Kona

If you do a Google search on "moving to the Big Island" with "jobs," you will find that most bloggers lament the lack of jobs here and tell you to bring your own, or create one for yourself. It's true.

Many of the jobs that ARE available are service sector jobs in hospitality and tourism, and do not pay very well. The average income for West Hawai'i is $50,000 and there are plenty of folks making less than twenty dollars an hour.

If you have a desirable skill or talent, you will most likely do well, IF you start to network as soon as you get here. Everyone will tell you—it's all about the relationships.

I left a job in Silicon Valley with a great salary, full benefits, and a huge network base. I thought I would be able to find a marketing position pretty easily when I arrived. After spending a year in Kona making ten dollars an hour working on a dolphin boat, and getting a few consulting jobs, I knew when I came back to move here full time I would have to have a better game plan.

When I arrived in Kona in 2010, I came with a part-time telecommuting job from San Mateo and a promise to myself that I would do it for a year. During that year, I networked as much as I could and I did things that got me noticed in the community, even if I did not make much money doing it. I put on social media training seminars and for a few of the sessions, gave the proceeds to charity; I applied for, and received, two County grants to offer social media training to business owners on the island to make it affordable for them to attend; I put on TechConKona with one of those grants to show my event planning and PR skills to the public; I joined the Chamber of Commerce and volunteered for their marketing committee; and I worked on the Big Island Chocolate Festival (for almost nothing) to develop it into a signature food festival that would supplement my income. I worked hard and it paid off. By the time my income from the Bay Area was cut off, I opened up my consulting business and started taking on clients who then knew me through word of mouth and my determination to succeed here.

Did I think it would be easier to get a 9 to 5 job? Yes! I thought about it, and after four years, I have seen VERY few good well-paying marketing positions open up. The ones I HAVE heard about were passed along the "coconut telegraph" before they became publicly available. This happens all the time. People want to see their friends and Ohana stay on the island, and will do what they can to help them before they help people they don't know from the mainland. UNLESS, you possess a skill that cannot be found easily here.

Talking Story—The Business Culture of Hawai'i
People want to talk story with you. Again, coming from the mainland, my MO was just to cut to the chase, be direct, and get the business aspect of the conversation handled. "Can you sponsor my event?" "How much is your marketing budget?" That approach does not work here. People want to know where you are from, who your mutual friends may be, and why you came to Kona. I had to spend hours talking story with my prospective clients to (thankfully) get their approval so they would work with me. Away from this island you may think that's a waste of time of billable hours. In Hawai'i? That's how business gets done.

I attended an event where the keynote speaker discussed the cultural differences of people on the mainland vs. those in Hawai'i and China. You will go far if you remember that in Hawai'i, business is done similarly to how it's done in Asia: utilizing connections and networks, unlike many businesses on the mainland, where people might cold call, door knock, and ask for your business without first having a relationship.

Job Listing Links
CraigsList
http://bit.ly/HawaiiCraigsList

Monster.com
http://bit.ly/MonsterKonaJobs

West Hawaii Today
http://bit.ly/WestHawaiiTodayJobs

Kamaʻāina Jobs
http://bit.ly/KamaainaJobs

Search the websites of major employers here on the island, including the hospitals, resorts, energy providers, and building industry.

Also, if you know how to use LinkedIn, www.LinkedIn.com, you can search for people who are doing business here in Hawaiʻi and start making those connections through that social network. I recently had a gentleman who had just moved here reach out to me via Linkedin—he had just gotten a public relations position at a large school here, and he wanted to learn more about the business community in Kona. Very clever.

A caveat to consider is that most employers want to see you living here before they will hire you, to make sure you know what you're getting into by moving here. Our next-door-neighbor's husband lives in Santa Cruz and has been looking for an Internet Technology job in West Hawaiʻi. There are people looking for his skills, but they want him to live here before they will hire him, which sets up a conundrum.

Quit his well paying job in California in the hopes he will get hired here, or stay put and hope someone will hire him first? This is a frequent issue. That's why so many people come here with nest eggs that will get them through the first few months.

If you DO plan on starting a business here, and plan to rely on the local labor force, I will give you a word of caution: Getting people to show up regularly for work is difficult. I was at a Chamber of Commerce event recently and the employers I spoke to about this book all said the same thing, "If we could just get people who wanted to work and were willing to show up consistently we would pay more, but we find ourselves with constant turnover and re-training issues." This is especially true in the restaurant business, although a friend said his administrative assistant called in sick and he found her on Facebook enjoying the beach and surfing with her friends. There is definitely a beach and surf culture going on here. Just be aware of it. If your kids get jobs, and they want to prosper here, tell them to not be flakes.

Here are links to help you start a new business in Hawai'i:
Hawai'i Business Express
> http://bit.ly/HawaiiBusinessExpress

Understanding Hawai'i's General Excise Tax
State of Hawai'i Department of Taxation
> http://tax.hawaii.gov/geninfo

Find out more about starting a business in Kona:
Hawai'i Small Business Development Center
> http://bit.ly/HawaiiSmallBusinessDevelopmentCenter
> (Mention to Hazel Beck, the Center Director, that I sent you.)

Chapter Twelve

Waves Will Kill You and
Other Ocean Safety Tips

Some people come to Hawai'i and think it's like Disneyland, with all of our beautiful places to see and fun things to do. However, unlike Disneyland, there are some dangerous places, and you won't see caution tape and red cones around them. Common sense prevails here, and Hawai'i can be dangerous if you are not alert, don't know the rules, or don't watch what other people who have lived here for a long time are doing.

Water Activities

When you live in Hawai'i, you may spend a lot of time in the water. Learning about the waves, geologic features, and sea creatures will go a very long way to keeping you, your children, and your guests safe.

Snorkeling

If you are new to snorkeling, do one of these two things:

Go to Kahaluu Beach Park in Keauhou. The whole bay is very shallow and you can see most of the tropical fish that reside in Hawai'i there. Kids can stand up on the sand and just put their faces in the water and view yellow tang, parrotfish, and a variety of wrasses.

This is a great place to make sure your equipment works, you know how to breathe, and you can see how you feel with the whole experience. You can also go out on some of the boats like *Fair Winds* or *The Body Glove* where you can jump into deeper water, you don't have to worry about standing on the coral or lava, and there are professionals to help you.

Jumping into deep water when you are not comfortable with snorkeling is a potential recipe for disaster. I have seen too many of my friends and their kids think they were ready to go off of "Two Step" near the Place of Refuge (Puʻuhonua oʻ Honaunau), only to freak out because of the deep water and the inability to stand up and readjust their equipment. They also had a hard time with the surge getting out of the water, and they were fighting with their equipment and fins. If you are going to live here for a while, take it easy and learn to snorkel correctly. Learn how to deal with issues like water in your breathing tube, your mask fogging up, or ill-fitting fins BEFORE you decide to take on some of the more challenging snorkel places on the island. Also, be careful of the wave surge when you are checking out shallow shelves. Hundreds of tropical fish like to swim in water that is less than twelve inches deep along the coral, which pulls you into finding them close to the rocks. A wave can come in and rake you across the coral, lava, and sea urchins if you are too close.

Kokua the Coral

As is the case at all places where you enjoy the ocean in Hawaiʻi, please remember to NOT step on the coral. Don't be that guy who told a tour friend of mine after being told to stop standing on the coral, "Why? I'll never be here again!" Those are the kinds of tourists that should be banned from Hawaiʻi. Forever. Our coral is some of the finest in the world, and only by protecting it can we be sure that our tropical fish and marine habitat stay pristine for future generations.

Beaches

When we first arrived in Kona, we headed to Magic Sands Beach on Aliʻi Drive. This beach is also called Disappearing Sands and White Sands. As soon as we stepped onto the beach, a man in his fifties was trying to get out of the water and he had a gash on his head and was holding his dislocated shoulder. We called 911 for him. Since then, we have seen an ambulance come to that beach more often than just about any other beach we've been to. Residents call that beach, "Tragic

Sands," "Magic Slams," and other names befitting a beach that has a shelf that throws up huge waves near the shore and throws you down onto the sand without much room to dive down to avoid it. Plus, it has hidden rocks. I can't state strongly enough—it is one of **the most dangerous beaches** in West Hawai'i, and one of the most beautiful. Watch other boogie boarders and body surfers for a while first. The large waves come in sets here. You can be playing in small waves for a few minutes and then four sets of six-foot waves can come in and crush you. This is especially something to be looking for if you have small children swimming in the break zone.

Another thing we see, shake our heads at, and wish someone would listen to: DO NOT turn your back to the ocean if you are anywhere near the wave zone. Also, DON'T stand there and let an eight-foot wave hit you and think *ducking* will work. I've seen this numerous times at Kua Bay and Magic Sands. When a wave hits you, hundreds of pounds of water are coming down on you, pushing and crushing you. Run at it and dive through it. If you are not bold enough to do that, don't be out in large surf. Lifeguards are not always on duty at White Sands, and there are none at Kua Bay. Act accordingly. Rogue waves can come and take you off of the rocks; so staying alert is key anywhere near the ocean.

Kayaking

Kayaks give you the freedom to do some discovery of lava tubes and caves, pulling up on remote areas, and wandering around on hidden beaches. I would recommend going out with experienced tour guides before going out on an extended tour alone. Wave surges can trap you in caves, and going up on land can expose you to getting cut up and hurt if hit by a wave, etc. I may be a Nervous Nellie, but seriously, go with a guide who knows the area and the rules.

Dangerous Marine Life

Cone Shell Mollusk

One very dangerous little Hawaiian creature that you are unlikely to hear about is the cone shell mollusk. This little snail-like creature lives in the ocean in a pretty little cone-shaped seashell. The danger with this marine animal lies in his shell. Children and adults who see this shell may be enticed to pick it up. (I learned about this through my daughter's Reef Teach program, and had not heard about it during the years I have lived here prior to that.)

The Cone Shell Mollusk has a little tendril that will shoot out and sting your hand, inflicting an incredibly painful sting that can be fatal. Cone shell mollusks are no reason to stay out of the ocean, but be careful which seashells you pick up from the ocean floor. If you are stung by a cone shell mollusk, seek medical attention immediately.

Man-O-War

The man-o-war is closely related to the jellyfish. They are unable to swim and will instead float on the surface of the water and let themselves be blown by the wind while their long tendrils hang down in the water. They have blue *sails* and come in on in-shore breezes.

When they wash up near the beach, they are likely to be unseen in the surf and can inflict stings to those who are walking along in the water and not paying attention. I have been stung at Hapuna Beach and so were dozens of others, so now I look on the sand to see if I see the blue sails and I check the wind pattern.

If one should sting you, people say urinating on it can treat the sting. The lifeguard at Hapuna had us all putting hot water on the stings. Ammonia and ammonia-based products such as Windex will also work. White vinegar is also a good cure. White vinegar can be used as a disinfectant that can be used on any minor scrapes and cuts.

Jellyfish

Jellyfish are not uncommon in Hawai'i, but you are unlikely to see them. (I have swum through a few jellyfish swarms while out swimming with dolphins, but did not get stung.) We DO have box jellyfish, but they are not the dangerous Australian box jellies you may have heard of. Still, they can inflict a painful sting.

Lionfish

Lionfish are beautifully striped brown and white or orange and white tropical fish with large protruding fan-shaped fins. These fish are poisonous and very dangerous, especially if you step on one accidentally, but they do not attack people.

Sea Urchins

Sea urchins, or *wana*, pronounced vana (the Hawaiian word for the purple sea urchin), are not poisonous, but if stepped on the spines go into your skin and can be excruciating. Be sure to watch your step when walking on submerged rocks in the ocean and wear water shoes until you get more familiar with the shoreline. They are not in the sand but ARE on the rocks and can be in the little nooks and crannies, so watch your hands too, especially when you are pulling yourself out of the water.

Keep Your Distance From Marine Life

You can get fined and jailed if you harass a sea turtle, dolphin, monk seal, or whale in Hawai'i. *West Hawaii Today* recently published a photo of a tourist straddling a Hawaiian sea turtle with a reminder to all that it is AGAINST THE LAW to come too close to our marine life. Please refrain from feeding, petting, touching, or chasing the animals that call Hawai'i home. Getting a selfie with a turtle is not only bad form, it can cost you in fines if you get turned in or caught.

Chapter Thirteen
Your New Friends:
Pests in Paradise

Depending upon your elevation, the foliage growing around your home, your proximity to dumpsters, and the amount of rain that can stand stagnant, you will be dealing with a variety of *pests*. Pests, of course, are more *pesty* depending upon your tolerance and patience for them. Just know that if you move to Kona, you have to deal with the fact that you moved to a tropical island. Tropical islands have residents other than people—some of which are native and some are not—that you can live with or you can't. These *neighbors* are another thing to consider, based upon where you want to live.

Centipedes

These are the worst. Some of our other insects or creatures are simply a nuisance. These guys sting. And they get into your bed, in your shoes, under your appliances, and are at the campgrounds. All places you find yourself barefoot, without a light, and vulnerable to them coming out at night to crawl around. DO NOT step on them, as they curl up backwards and can sting you that way. I have seen a few down at our condo complex and my friends up *mauka*, surrounded by tropical foliage, see them more frequently. They are very quick, so while you stand there and scream, they will be making a beeline for under your bed. The stings of the red centipedes tend to be the least painful and the stings of the more rare neon blue centipedes are the worst. Blue centipedes rarely grow to a large size, so if you see one of the larger bugs, it will most likely be the red variety. People have reported seeing centipedes of up to a foot long! If you want to avoid them getting into bed with you, skip using bed skirts.

Cockroaches

Down where I live, near the golf course and in a condo environment, we get our two-and-a-half inch-flying cockroach buddies. They don't breed in our homes; they breed in the fertile and moist grounds of the golf course. We discovered this when we first moved here and found ourselves walking the golf course after a fantastic sunset near Kanaloa. We were at the base of a hill where water flows down and makes it an especially nice place for insects, and we saw dozens of cockroaches emerging from the grass. Screaming aside, we were educated in etymology pretty quickly. Our cat likes to bring them into our home and play with them. They are attracted to light and enjoy getting through broken screens and open doors. The good news is that they don't bite, although they fly, which can be VERY disconcerting to our new residents and guests. My husband has gotten so used to them now, he simply picks them up and throws them against the wall, stunning them, and then takes them outside.

Coqui Frogs

Coqui frogs were accidentally brought to the island from Puerto Rico or the mainland about thirty years ago and started their invasion in Puna. They are dime-sized little amphibians that need moisture in their environment to live, so you won't find them in the lava fields or other dry environments like Kohala. SOME neighborhoods in Kona have them, but most of us, upon hearing even one little sound of "ko-kee!" will track the buggers down and feed them to the nearest chicken. Before settling into a new home, listen to the neighborhood after dark. The frogs are the loudest in the summer months. We were camping in Kalopa campground at 2,000 feet above sea level, near Honokaa, and it sounded like an arena of screaming fans. That's how loud they are.

Geckos

Some people consider the Madagascar green geckos to be pests. Personally, I like them because they don't bite, they stay out of my way, and they eat the insects in our home. They are beautiful green, blue, and red lizard-like creatures and we have been entertained for hours at dinner watching them compete with each other to catch and eat gnats, mosquitos, small cockroaches, and sometimes, each other. They DO poop *down* the walls, so most people would rather they live outside. We have had tenants who HATE them, and do strange things like putting out mothballs. That does not work. If you don't like geckos, you may be in trouble, as they are all over Kona.

Mice and Rats

Rats love dumpsters and they love fun places to hide and breed. I have not seen many mice in Kona, but they are all over the homes up on the Kohala Coast. Call an exterminator.

Mongoose

If you see these wily little beady-eyed, squirrel-like creatures, just leave them alone. They won't come in your house, come up to you, or do much besides get into your garbage, if you leave it outside your door. They like to live with the feral cat population where they get good meals, and the cats leave them alone because they are notoriously vicious. I learned this first-hand when I chased one into a hole and it turned around and hissed at me with little fangs. Remember, they kill cobras. Speaking of cobras, did you know that there are no snakes on Hawai'i Island? They are illegal to bring here because of the devastating effect they would have on our local bird population. The mongoose story claims that people brought this cat-like creature onto Hawai'i Island to deal with the rats, which had hitched rides on the merchant ships. However, the rats are nocturnal and the mongooses sleep at night, making it so that neither the twain shall meet. (You will find, after spending time here, other stories of creatures being brought onto the island to combat an invasive pest and you just have to say "what were they thinking?")

Spiders

We have a few different kinds of spiders, but the only one that is truly poisonous is the brown recluse, and it's pretty rare in regular neighborhoods. Farms, shacks, and sheds are more likely to have these. One spider we have here that can scare you simply by its size is the cane spider. It's huge, and likes to hide out in dark places, mostly up *mauka*.

Mosquitos

These are just about anywhere there is any water, and they are more prevalent when we have our rainy season in the summer. Avoid inadvertently breeding them by having bromeliads around your property, where mosquitos can breed in the water caught in the cups of that plant. My friend developed a great solution to the mosquito issue by inventing Mosquito Magik, which you can find in most of the health food stores on the island. I hate these guys just as much as I hate the centipedes!

Fire Ants

A relative newcomer to Kona, the fire ant's sting burns strongly and itches intensely for weeks, and they pose a potential danger through allergic reactions. Brought to the island accidentally through tropical plants, and originally found in Puna, they now can be found in Kona. Be careful when deciding to sit down on the grass at the large ball fields, as they are drawn to moisture and shade. My friend Lance was recently bitten all over his body when he wrapped himself in an ant-infested towel. *West Hawaii Today* did a story about this new invasion recently: http://bit.ly/FireAntsInWestHawaii

Feral Pigs

This *pest* is more for those of you who may be thinking about buying a farm or land up *mauka*. The little buggers like to tear up the soil looking for food and water and if you come across a momma and her babies, watch out, they attack. We had a chance to see how destructive they are on a variety of hikes, and they have been disastrous for many of the native plants in Hawai'i. I have one word for these guys: *Imu*. They make fantastic pulled pork.

Mynah and Franklin Birds

These birds are so loud that if you have them nesting near your house, you will NEVER sleep in past sunrise. And when the sunrise is at 5:30 a.m., it gets a bit annoying. When the sun has been up for about thirty minutes, they disperse, but by then you are awake. They also enjoy any pet food left outside. A side note on the Mynah birds—they hop all over the roads. You will think you are going to hit them, and just as you are about to swerve, they move.

Chapter Fourteen

Living and Shopping Options in West Hawai'i

Singles Living

Meetup Groups

There are a variety of Meetup groups in Kona offering everything from hiking and adventures, to writing/spirituality, to creating fun ways to hang out and get to know people:

http://bit.ly/KonaMeetUpGroup

Online dating

Online dating can be tough here. Check out the folks who are looking at this free online singles site:

http://bit.ly/KonaPersonalAds

Bars and Live Entertainment

Quite a few of my single friends hang out at **Humpy's** and like to attend the many events they hold there:

http://bit.ly/1vGjlYH

Henry Kapono plays at **Don's the Beachcomber at the Royal Kona Resort** the last Thursday of the month and he's a big draw with the over-forty singles crowd. Some of my single friends also like to go to **Huggo's** to dance and listen to the entertainment.

http://bit.ly/HuggosEntertainment

There is also free entertainment next door at **On the Rocks**, and though there is no defined dance floor (because it is a sand pit!), it's VERY fun on weekend nights!

Laverne's Sports Bar used to be Lulu's. Looking for a way to meet sports-minded individuals? You might like to come here, where people cheer and blow horns when a team scores.

http://bit.ly/LavernesKona

Community Volunteer Groups

A single friend of mine mentioned, "You are going to get what you get when you hang out in Kona bars." Volunteers who are entrenched in the community, who lend their time and/or lead community organizations in Kona, KNOW PEOPLE. They get to you know you through watching your involvement, you ask for introductions to their single friends, and you may have a very nice connection. This recently worked well for a teacher friend of mine!

Senior Living

If you are thinking about retiring here or bringing an aging parent, the only full-service retirement and assisted living facility in Kona is the Regency at Hualalai. Good news is they allow pets.

http://bit.ly/RegencyHualalai

In early 2014, *West Hawaii Today* reported that developers are looking at creating a senior living development off of Kuakini. There are hundreds of seniors needing skilled nursing and assisted living in Kona. Development can be slow in Kona, so the 350 jobs it will bring, along with the affordable housing it's proposing to offer, may be a ways off, but there IS a plan:

http://bit.ly/AffordableSeniorHousing

For Those Who Love to Shop: Shopping Malls

If you LOVE to shop, Kona may not be the exact fit for you, as we have limited shopping malls, but we DO have a variety of shops and centers, allowing you to find what you need, and spend some time browsing and shopping. Many of the malls, both in Kona and out at the resorts, have an active calendar of events, with festivals, races, small

Farmer's Markets, Hawaiian cultural demonstrations, and hula events. Here are the sites, so you can see what our "shopping scene" looks like!

Kona

Kona Commons
http://bit.ly/KonaCommons

Lanihau Center
http://bit.ly/LanihauCenter

Kona International Marketplace
http://bit.ly/KonaInternationalMarket

Keauhou Village Shopping Center
http://bit.ly/KeauhouVillageShops

Makalapua Center
This center has movie theaters and a small Macy's and Kmart

Kohala Coast

Kings Shops
http://bit.ly/KingsShops

Queens Shops
http://bit.ly/QueensMarketPlace

The Shops at Mauna Lani
http://bit.ly/ShopsAtMaunaLani

Hilo

Prince Kuhio Plaza
Real life, enclosed shopping mall:
http://bit.ly/PrinceKuhioPlaza

For the Do-it-Yourselfers: Building Supply Places
When we first bought our condo, we had to take it down to the studs. We spent A LOT of time doing renovation work and went to these businesses for what we needed. A few of these businesses also have great landscaping supplies and plants:

Lowe's
http://bit.ly/LowesKona
75-5677 Hale Kapili St, Kailua-Kona, HI 96740

Home Depot
http://bit.ly/HomeDepotKona
73-5598 Olowalu St, Kailua-Kona, HI 96740

HPM
http://bit.ly/HPM
74-5511 Luhia St, Kailua-Kona, HI 96740

Honsador Lumber Building Construction
http://bit.ly/Honsador
73-5580 Kauhola St, Kailua-Kona, HI 96740

Ace Hardware
http://bit.ly/AceHardwareKona
74-5500 Kaiwi St, Kailua-Kona, HI 96740

Kona is a small town. You keep seeing people around town and start-making conversation and then they pop up at business, community, and social events. The more you get out doing what you like, the more you see the same people. The other side of the sword is that Kona is a small town. A very small town. As Maya Angelou stated, "I've learned that people will forget what you said, people will forget what you did, but people will never forget how you made them feel." Hint: Carry your Aloha Spirit with you when you are conducting yourself around town, and know that people like to talk story.

Chapter Fifteen

Eight Ways to Save Money as a *Kamaʻāina*

1) Get a Costco Card

If you shop in bulk, you'll find this will save on your monthly grocery bill, and while you're there, Costco has the cheapest price on gas too.

What I eat: I suggest getting the wheat bread, which can cost seven dollars a loaf in the grocery store, and the yogurt, which will cost $1.60 a piece at KTA. The six-dollar Rotisserie chicken is a household staple in Kona, as is the pizza. (You can pick up a "U Bake It" pizza for parties and such for less than $10.) My friends say the hummus, cheese, Mountain Thunder coffee, and mac nuts are cheaper than at other grocery stores. Another interesting thing to note is that you can sometimes get REALLY good deals on patio and other household furniture, including beach chairs, umbrellas, and party tables.

Bulk suggestions: Be careful when buying in bulk on breakfast cereals and crackers. The humidity will make dry items go stale unless you put them in airtight containers or store them in the fridge. Also, you will find that cutting down on your fetish for packaged and processed items that need to be shipped here will save you in the long run on most island grocery store products and help keep extra rubbish out of our landfill, too.

Not to disparage Costco, but I would suggest buying your fruits, veggies, milk, eggs, and meat locally. Fruit at Costco does not ripen correctly and has a tendency to rot faster. We grow it here, why not take advantage of fresh and sustainable?

2) Get Familiar With the Farmers Markets

The Keauhou Farmers market at the Keauhou Shopping Center is held in their parking lot on Saturday mornings from *8 a.m. to 12 p.m.* They have a variety of coffee farmers, vegetable/fruit tables, homemade breads, jams, honey, and other locally sourced products. You can also buy orchids, flowers, and crafts.

http://bit.ly/KeauhouFarmersMarket

On Saturday mornings, from *8 a.m. to 12 p.m.,* check out the Homestead Farmers Market in Waimea. This market has some of the most famous producers on the island, including Hamakua mushrooms, WOW tomatoes, Big Island Goat Cheese, and strawberries. Many of the chefs on the island shop directly from this farmers market.

http://bit.ly/WaimeaFarmersMarket

If you plan on being in Waimea for the Homestead Farmers Market, also check out the Parker School Farmers Market from *7:30 a.m. to 12 p.m.*

http://bit.ly/WaimeaTownMarket

Another good one is the South Kona Green Market at Amy Greenwell's Botanical Gardens. This market is a scene! People from South Kona come for breakfast items and fresh brewed Kona coffee, and they shop and hang out. It's held at 82-6188 Mamalahoa Hwy in Captain Cook. *9 a.m. to 2 p.m.*

http://bit.ly/SouthKonaMarket

For farm products, local crafts, and food vendors, check out the Ho'oulu Community Farmer's Market every Wednesday at the Sheraton Kona Resort and Spa at Keauhou Bay. *9 a.m. to 2 p.m.*

http://bit.ly/HoouluFarmersMarket

All the markets allow for you to meet the farmers, coffee producers, bakers, fishermen, and the folks who supply amazing local products from our land and their hand. Ask for tastes, many of the vendors
love to turn people on to new tropical fruits like dragon fruit, rambu-
tan, breadfruit, and the numerous varieties of avocados and mangos we
have here. The line for the fresh fish starts at *7 a.m.* at the Keauhou
Market, so get there to enjoy fresh-caught mahi mahi, ahi, ono, ʻopelu,
and yellow fin.

3) Find the Cool Happy Hours

Four-dollar pupus and six-dollar drinks at Huggos on the Rocks, from
3 p.m. to 5 p.m., is one of my favorites. The sliders, fish tacos, and
nachos are only four dollars and you can enjoy wine, beer, Mai Tais,
and Green Flashes for six dollars while you put your feed in the sand
and enjoy the sunset.

http://bit.ly/HuggosOnRocks

This is key when your friends show up and you want to go watch
the sunset, listen to live entertainment, watch some hula, all of which
you can do for under fifty dollars. You treat THEM and then suggest
Jackie Rey's when it's their turn to treat you!

Another great happy hour is Kenichi Pacific at the Keauhou Shopping Center. They have 50 percent-off sushi from *5 p.m. to 6:30 p.m.*
at their bar. You have to get there early to get a seat, but it's worth it
for the sushi and hand rolls.

http://bit.ly/KenichiPacific

Kona Brewery, Outback Steakhouse, Don's The Beachcomber Mai
Tai bar, Sam Choy's Kai Lanai, and Bite Me Fish Market all have great
happy hour pricing. Check out more here, thanks to Yelp:

http://bit.ly/YelpRecommendations

4) Get Your Driver's License

Get into the DMV soon after you arrive so you can enjoy *Kamaʻāina* rates. Some of the activities in Kona such as the Fair Wind Cruises and many of the hotels and restaurants give the locals a nice price break, ranging from between 10 and 20 percent off. Sometimes the tours/activities will extend the rate to others in your party, making you a hero to your visiting friends and family. If you are dining out, enjoying activities or services, just ask to see if they have a *Kamaʻāina* rate.

5) Sign up for Emails From Hawaiian Airlines

Be the first to see airfare deals, so you can alert your friends and family when they have a big airfare sale.

http://bit.ly/HawaiianAirlines

6) For the Kids, Go See Movies on Tuesdays

Get a deal at the Keauhou Regal Cinema at the Keauhou Shopping Center on Tuesdays. They have one-dollar hot dogs and two-dollar popcorn, and if you get there early, there's a matinee discount. Get a Regal Club Card and you get **free** movies, popcorn, and drinks pretty regularly.

http://bit.ly/RegalCinemasKona

7) Get it to Go!

Get slices of pizza at Bianelli's Pizza at Keauhou Shopping Center for two dollars each, drinks to go, and watch the sunset on the beach at White Sands. This is our favorite "affordable dinner night" for our family and we get a great bang for the buck with the kids and our visiting friends.

You can do this with take-out sushi from KTA, You Make It Roll, and L&L Hawaiian BBQ. For you discerning foodies, go to Da Poke Shack on Aliʻi Drive http://dapokeshack.com/Menu.html, or Umeke's in downtown Kona and buy a variety of *poke* and have a *poke* fest. (That's *poke*, pronounced pokee, like hokey pokey. It means, cut in Hawaiian, and it's cut up and cubed fresh fish with shoyu marinade. Da Poke Shack is Zagat-rated, and for even more adventurous poke lovers, try Umeke's, across the street from the Kona library downtown. As the locals say, "Broke da Mouth" grinds.)

8) Beach it

Buy a BBQ grill, six-foot table, shade tent, beach chairs, ice chest, and a pretty tablecloth. Boom. You'll start meeting other people at beaches all over West Hawai'i while taking in a great view, grilling your own local meats and veggies, and getting out of the house. Isn't this why you want to move to Hawai'i?

Chapter Sixteen

Interesting Facts the Locals Know About Your New Island Home

Here are a few bonus things I am going to share with you that will make living life here a bit easier, or at least give you some food for thought about moving and living here successfully.

Road Issues

Mile Markers

Getting around is pretty easy. Kona is laid out like a grid. We only have a few major roads, so if you know to look for the mile markers, it gives you a good idea of where you are and how to find places. Since we have VERY few road signs, the locals know to use the mile marker system to say where they live, play, and work. For instance, when there is a traffic accident, the radio station will tell you that the accident occurred between mile marker 101 and 102. You know then to avoid that section in South Kona. A variety of tour books will also use mile markers to alert you to cool places. My friend John Heatherington created this map with the overlays of the mile markers so you can see the whole island and the roadways with the mile markers:

http://bit.ly/MileMarkerMap

Speed Traps

When you drive into downtown Kona coming north, there is a speed limit sign that says "15 MPH" right near the Royal Kona Resort. Right next to that is a place where Kona's finest can hang out with speed guns. Slow down. They also hang out up on the hill and can look into your car to see if you are wearing a seat belt or are on your cell phone. This is the place to put away all distractions and pay attention. Tourists are crossing the road, running, biking, and skating. Besides, you can go slow and enjoy the vibe as you travel through downtown.

When you are traveling down the Queen K after you pass Maka-lupua, it appears to be a wide-open road and you can go nuts. Not so! The speed limit is thirty-five for a block then forty-five out to the air-port, not fifty-five, and the police like to keep an eye on this section.

The locals will often flash their lights at you if there is a police car parked ahead of you that they have just passed. That's a nice gesture of the Aloha spirit!

Refrain from going over sixty-five mph on the Queen K to the Kohala Coast. There are MANY traffic accidents on this island due to the ease of being able to cross the center divide and plow into an on-coming car. Since the road is a single lane, people take risks on passing all the time. Be vigilant.

Traffic

I used to sit in eight-lane traffic in the Bay Area for miles. It's not like that, but again, with two-lane roads, it can be just as frustrating. During the school year, and especially when all the tourists are in town in the winter, you will crawl from Kam III to Makalapua from 7:45 a.m. to 9:00 a.m. Lately, they've been building a new extension from Queen K to Ali'i Drive, which makes matters worse.

If you can avoid heading south from Henry St. to Kam III Rd on the Queen K between 4:00 and 5:30 p.m., do so. If you hate sitting in traffic, you can take Ali'i Drive, and watch the ocean as you travel about twenty-five mph, or you can take the upper highway, Mala-mahoa, and subject yourself to a twisty turning road through pretty coffee farm territory. We avoid morning traffic on the Queen K from Kam III Rd to Kealekekua by taking the Hokulia Bypass road, which you take by continuing south on Ali'i Drive past Keauhou. That road pops you up near the McDonalds, cutting off about ten minutes from taking the usual Highway 11 route. They are working on extending the Hokulia bypass road all the way to Napo'opo'o Road for quick access to Kealekua Bay and South Kona.

Traveling from the airport to Kona on Friday afternoons can seem grueling. Leave extra time and play your music loud and sing!

Practice the Aloha Spirit While Driving

Take it easy on the roads. Local custom states to not speed up when a car is passing you. That's an accident waiting to happen. Flash your lights to let oncoming drivers who are trying to make a left turn know you are slowing down to allow them to make the turn in front of you. Also, let drivers into traffic from driveways and side roads, and don't try to cut them off. We don't do honking here, either.

Lava

There are two main types of lava in Hawai'i: *pahoehoe* (pa-hoy-hoy) and *a'a* (ah-ah). The crunchy lava you see in most of Kona is *a'a*. *A'a* lava is the most common type of lava, which cools down, forming fragmented, rough, sometimes spiny, or blocky surfaces. The other kind of lava is *pahoehoe*, meaning ropy or to paddle (probably from the swirls on the water's surface), in Hawaiian. I bring this up for a few reasons: Many rock walls use *a'a* lava and they build them to be exactly at your bumper level, where you cannot see them. When you back into the walls, which eventually you will, the lava will poke a hole into your car. It's called a "lava bite."

I warn you now so you can try to keep your car bite free, because left unrepaired, you'll also see how fast things rust due to our ocean air.

The second reason I bring it up is that most mainlanders have not practiced their balancing skills in walking over uneven terrain, which includes lava that appears not only near the ocean, but on our trails, in landscaping, and parking lots, etc. Small children especially seem to have a hard time when they first come here and get plenty of banged up and scraped knees, or worse. Second to the kids getting hurt, adults who don't watch their step are at risk. Lava is EVERYWHERE on this island. Wear sturdy shoes and bring Band-Aids.

If you decide to walk over a lava field in an attempt to discover something fun like a beach or lava tube, be aware that lava conducts heat and is HOT in the afternoon. We learned this from an ill-fated attempt to reach a lagoon as we walked from the highway to the ocean when we ran out of water. We ended up extremely dehydrated. I keep talking about common sense in this book, but sometimes the lure of something fun makes you skip thinking. Why do you think I wrote this book? So you can avoid OUR mistakes!

Talk Story

When folks here in Hawai'i spend some time getting to know each other, gossip, and discuss life, it's called "talking story." This is what people who live here will do with you when you slow down and ask them questions about their island home and what they have learned here. You'll learn and appreciate more if you talk story and ask about history, legends, culture, agriculture, and why they came here, etc. Talking story is really the only way relationships are built here, so grab a chair.

If you are talking story to a long-time Hawaiian resident, you may find that they insert Pidgin into the conversation. Hawaiian Pidgin originated on sugar plantations as a form of communication used between English speaking and non-English speaking immigrants, and natives in Hawai'i. Other immigrants who came to work the land further influenced this Hawaiian Creole. When we first arrived, we were watching a TV commercial and they were talking about "choke" lights. I had no idea there was an underlying language spoken here. When I first heard a friend with a pidgin accent, I thought she was from Minnesota!

Pidgin has some interesting nuances and the history is very interesting. Learn more through this link to Wikipedia:
http://bit.ly/HawaiianPidgin

Get your Pidgin on, or at least understand what your new friends may be saying using this Pidgin dictionary:
http://bit.ly/PidginDictionary

Technology

If you come with all your tech toys, you'll need to know a few things. We do NOT have an Apple store here. I made a few new friends who can fix your broken screens and diagnose the issues, but for a new iPhone or iPad, you'll have to shop at the Apple store in Waikiki, on the island of Oahu. There are a few Mac specialists here (Mac Made Easy) and many people get their tech toy fix at Walmart, Target, or MacNet.

Speaking of technology, there are a few restaurants that are not fond of you speaking on your cell phone on premises. Banks and libraries will tell you point blank to turn them off when entering. You generally don't see groups of young professionals huddled around a lunch table texting, tweeting, and Facebooking while barely talking to each other in Kona, which is a nice break from the mainland. (Unless you are in Starbucks, which is a weird satellite space to the mainland!)

I will admit that I use my iPhone to take photos and blog on Facebook, but I try and keep it to a minimum. However, IF you enjoy social networking, we have a few people who have put up some good info on Foursquare to help you with tips at many restaurants and points of interest. http://bit.ly/FourSquareSocialChannel

Check into the playgrounds and bowling alley and you'll see my photos. (Many local restaurants and businesses have specials and discounts if you "check in." Join FourSquare to get the free french fries at Ultimate Burger.)

I thought Kona would grasp technology better when I first arrived four years ago, and I was training business owners on using social media channels for marketing and relationship building. It was during this time that I learned how important face-to-face, old-fashioned relationship building is. There's room for both, and I have stayed connected with hundreds of friends on the mainland using social media. Besides, you need to have a Facebook or Instagram account to show everyone the photos of your new life in Kona, right?

Thrift Stores

There are at least six local thrift and consignment shops in/near Kona. Right near downtown, as of this writing there are: Memory Lane, Goodwill Industries, Salvation Army, the Kona Outdoor Circle (look up Sadie Seymore Botanical Garden), and my favorite in Kealekekua: King's Daughters Ministry.

For furniture, check out the Habitat for Humanity REStore near Costco and "The Second Hand" in Kealekekua.

These stores are wonderful for getting jackets, if you need to outfit your visiting friends when it's time to go visit Volcano or Mauna Kea. We also get great deals on tropical print dresses, shirts, and kids' knick knacks, and really, do your beach chairs or back yard furniture have to be brand new?

Useful Fun Facts:

- The state fish of Hawai'i is the humuhumunukunukuapua'a, also known as the reef triggerfish. It is the only reef fish that has bitten me. Twice. One attacked my husband and father-in-law recently, as well. Avoid pointing at them.
- The ukulele, considered to be a Hawaiian invention, was actually brought to the islands by the Portuguese. Ukulele means "jumping flea," and was so named because the fast moving strumming of the hand while playing looked like a dog scratching.
- Hawaiian shirts are a product of the 19th century and began when missionaries gave the Hawaiians plain shirts to cover their bare chests. The Hawaiians painted the shirts to make them more attractive.

Here are a few more you may enjoy reading about:
http://bit.ly/50ThingsToKnowAbout

Information for Families

Chapter Seventeen

School Guide for West Hawai'i

If you are a family moving to Kona, you should definitely be thinking about your child's future education and what you are willing to do for his or her educational goals.

As with many desirable towns across the country, the schools with the best scores are the most sought after, and homes in that area are some of the least affordable. Giving your child an amazing education in Kona needs planning and patience, or a pocketbook.

Public Schools in West Hawai'i

The public junior and senior high schools in the West Hawai'i district are Kealekehehe and Konawaeana. If you live south of Walua Road (which is basically a mile south of Kona), your kids will be attending Konawena Junior High or Senior High, located in South Kona, south of the Kona Community Hospital.

If you live north of Walua, your child will attend Kealekehe Intermediate and Senior High School.

I am going to say that I know parents whose children have attended both schools and have faced some of the same issues that secondary schools across the country face with their student body and teachers. I'll also point out that some kids go on from our high schools to top-notch colleges throughout the country. I'll say a few things in support of both, and you can learn more online from students, parents, and teachers who attend those schools.

Public High Schools

Konawaena High School

This school's campus is older and Konawaena used to be the only junior and senior high for ALL the children in West Hawai'i. The two-lane road to get there in the morning and at afternoon pick-up is very congested, even now, with only half the population sending their kids there. They have a strong athletics program and the spirit in the area for the football team is incredible.

http://www.konawaenahs.org

Kealekekehe High

This high school has a relatively new campus, located straight up from the Honokohau Harbor. The robotics team is one of the best in the state and has competed nationally. They have some fantastic facilities, including a full car shop, TV and art studios, and a commercial kitchen for the culinary students.

http://www.khswaveriders.org

Public Elementary Schools

Kahakai Elementary

My son and daughter attended this school for a few months before being accepted into the public charter school they now attend. Unlike some of the local charter schools, Kahakai has the funding for special education teachers. The DOE states that Kahakai "is an official science, technology, engineering and math (STEM) school." They have a computer lab, and my daughter had an excellent math experience there. Check the website for exact school boundaries.

http://bit.ly/KahakaiElementary

Kealakehe Elementary

This school is located off of Palani Road, up *mauka* from downtown. Their mission "is to provide a quality education that meets the academic, social, creative, emotional and physical needs of all students, in a safe, nurturing environment."

http://bit.ly/KealekeheElementary

Holualoa Elementary

The school is located in the desirable *arts* town of Holualoa, which is located at about the 1,000-foot elevation range, a mile up from Kona, and surrounded by coffee farms and plantations. Known for its tough academic policies, Holualoa "sets clear, measurable targets that are ambitious and challenging," as their site says. The housing market in that area is very desirable.

http://bit.ly/HolualoaElementary

Konawaena Elementary

The school is located in South Kona, in the heart of the Kona coffee area, on the green slopes of Hualalai. The school is "committed to ensuring all students graduate college and [are] career-ready through effective use of standards-based education," according to their site.

http://bit.ly/KonawaenaElementary

Charter Schools in West Hawai'i

Kona has seen the development of some very good charter schools. They all have a waiting list. If your plan is to move to Kona and get right into one of these schools, heads up on this. There is either a lottery system or waiting list at each one.

Kona Pacific Public Charter School: Grades K-8

Our kids have attended this school for four years. The school is situated on forty acres of land in South Kona, above the Kona Community Hospital, and selects students based on a lottery system. The school offers a Waldorf-based curriculum, interspersed with Hawaiian culture and agricultural sustainability. My children enjoy playing in the bamboo forest and spending time in the large gardens, where they learn about working with the land and respecting the *'āina*. "The curriculum offers a holistic, hands-on, project-based education inspired by Waldorf education, promoting student achievement in language arts, math, science, visual arts, musical training and movement."

http://bit.ly/KonaPacificPublicCharter

Innovations Public Charter School: Grades K-8
The list to get into this charter school, located almost directly above downtown Kona, is long. Founded in 2001, Innovations has a great reputation in town as a strong academic school. "IPCS is best known for its student centered learning in multi-age groupings, inquiry and project-based focus, thematic integrative curriculum, arts and technology integration, parent participation, and its caring and experienced staff."

http://bit.ly/InnovationsCharter

West Hawai'i Explorations Academy: Middle School: Grades 6-8 and High School: Grades 9-12
West Hawai'i Explorations Academy, or WHEA, is located near the Natural Energy Lab and the Ocean Thermal Energy Conversion (OTEC) area, near the Kona Airport, and within hundreds of feet of the Pacific Ocean, giving it a decidedly marine and technology sciences focus. WHEA also has a strong robotics team and is known for not having a "normal" classroom environment. The school will have to relocate within the next few years as it is negatively affected by the planned airport expansion and is in the tsunami inundation zone. Plans are to expand the school, which is good, as WHEA is also a sought-after educational experience for students wishing to pursue careers in the marine and oceanography fields. This school offers a project-based and individual study program.

http://bit.ly/West Explorations

Private Schools

University of the Nations: Pre-School

If you are coming with young children, this pre-school is highly regarded and located near downtown. They have a terrific educational and fun environment. You'll need to apply early for this much sought-after program.

http://bit.ly/UniversityofNationsKona

Makua Lani Christian Academy

Located on Palani Road, a few minutes up *mauka* from downtown, Makua Lani Christian Academy hosts its lower grades of K-7. The "lower campus," as they call it, offers a Christian-based education for grades 8 through 12.

http://bit.ly/KonaChristianAcademy

The Academy just recently became the owner of the former Hualalai Academy campus, located at 74-4966 Kealakaa St. The fourteen-acre campus can accommodate between 250 and 300 students. *West Hawaii Today* reported that the Board President said, "The school is an amazing facility with which we can further serve the needs of affordable, private education in West Hawai'i."

http://bit.ly/MakuLaniChristian

Hawai'i Preparatory Academy

HPA, as this elite school is known, is actually located in Waimea, about an hour north of Kona. It is the most expensive and is one of the finest private schools on the Big Island. "The mission of the Hawai'i Preparatory Academy is to provide exceptional learning opportunities and a diverse community honoring the traditions of Hawai'i." Students can board in dorms at Hawai'i Preparatory Academy, starting in 6th grade. My daughter begs me regularly to attend this school. It's like a college campus and offers an amazing array of educational and sports opportunities. Graduating HPA students routinely go to the best colleges in the nation. Some Kona students take a school bus to HPA to avoid having to board. (I am hoping this book does exceptionally well so I can grant my child's wish!)

http://bit.ly/PrepAcademy

Parker School

Also located in Waimea, Parker School offers a rigorous college preparatory experience coupled with a wide range of extracurricular offerings. In 2014, a Parker School senior was selected as a Presidential Scholar, the second year in a row that this has occurred. Numerous national merit finalists have been Parker School students over the past decade. Performing arts are extremely popular at the school, with numerous plays and musicals performed every year in the vintage theatre. Parker is the only school on the Big Island with an interscholastic speech and debate team, producing many state champions and national tournament qualifiers. A variety of interscholastic sports teams are offered, as well as recreational league teams for middle and lower school students. And all this in a supportive, small school environment! Parker School graduates attend many of America's finest universities. Approximately 50% of all Parker School students take advantage of the institution's extensive financial aid resources.

http://bit.ly/ParkerSchoolWaimea

There are quite a few families that have chosen an alternative schooling option by either utilizing online educational programs or home schooling. Friends of ours home-school their children, and then frequently have "field trips," where the kids can interact with other children while they explore the cultural and geographical diversity of Hawai'i. This works really well for many families, including a family we know who lives in Ocean View, a good hour's drive from Kona.

I wanted to also share something special that is taking place in many of the schools on our island. The schools are using locally grown fruits and veggies in their breakfast and lunch programs and most schools in Hawai'i have their own school gardens, as well. The opportunity to taste exotic and tropical fruits, while enjoying all the health benefits of having fruits and vegetables available for snacks and meals, has been a real plus to our kids. Here's an article *West Hawaii Today* did about the USDA funding the programs in our schools:

http://bit.ly/USDAProgramBringsFreshProduce

Chapter Eighteen
Safe Keiki Beaches Near Kona

"Where can my four-year-old play safely on an island filled with sharp lava?" "Where can I let my five-year-old explore, without worrying about him getting hit by monster waves?"

These are a few of the questions I get all the time. Here are the top three safest and most popular beaches for families, but first, a word of caution. Make sure your children always remember that the rocks near the water can be slippery and SHARP. Watch out for sea urchins, especially the purples ones that locally are called *wana* by Hawaiians. If you step on them, or get washed into them, it's beyond painful. Children should be cautioned to never stick their fingers or feet into the spaces between rocks underwater. If your children DO step on the sea urchins, the spines break off into their skin and cannot be removed. Put vinegar on the wound. There is not much else you can do. It takes about a week for the pain to go away. My husband stepped directly on a *wana* before going into the water to snorkel and was in extreme pain for hours—it took over a month to heal completely. Have your children wear water shoes, which give them protection against the *wana* AND can offer traction on the algae covered rocks.

1. **Kukio "keiki" beach** — A public beach, five miles north of the Kona International Airport, is located just outside the private, gated community of Kukio. That means you have to check in with security guard shack to enter. There are also limited parking spaces, twenty-seven to be exact, so if you are planning on going, carpool and go early. This is one of the few public beaches where you will find soap, paper towels, and clean restrooms (go figure, it's in the neighborhood with the billionaires, so it's a nice amenity that Kona beaches don't see often

enough). The swimming area is ideal for keikis and toddlers, with little wave action. For the older kids and adults, there is a bay to the right of the little keiki lagoon that has excellent snorkeling. But beware—there's a drop off at the end of the lagoon that scared the heck out of me. I wrote a post about it, too! http://bit.ly/AdventureAtTheDropOff

The walk from the parking lot to the beach is approximately fifty yards of paved sidewalk. Be sure to stay on the path, due to Hawaiian sensitivity issues. Security is constantly monitoring the area. (Again, because Michael Dell and other financial luminaries live nearby!)

2. **Kona Keiki Ponds** — This is another gathering spot for families with small children, especially when West Hawai'i beaches are closed due to high surf. The ponds are located behind the public swimming pool near downtown Kona. Look for the football field behind the community pool, park there, and walk across the field to find the path that leads to the beach. This hidden beach is in front of a variety of vacation homes. You can also see that there are not many trees for shade. Bring beach umbrellas. Kids love to float around here with their toys and there's plenty of exploring to do here.

3. **Kahalu'u Beach Park** in Keauhou is great for kids to learn how to snorkel and play at the water's edge. The entire bay is not more than eight feet deep and makes for a nice way for parents to stand up, while helping their kids in the water with their masks and fins. You will see just about every type of tropical fish located in Hawai'i in this bay. There are picnic tables, BBQ pits, and a pavilion for shade there. Located about five miles south of downtown Kona, it has an excellent Reef Teach program for all ages. There are a lot of green sea turtles to show the kids, as well. Please remember: enter the water near the Life Guard station and WATCH other people getting in. There's a *trench* that you follow to get into the bay. Walking across the rocks to jump in is DANGEROUS; I've seen many tourists slip and fall there. They now have some volunteers for "Reef Teach," who are doing their best to

stand there to guard the turtles, make sure people don't step all over the coral, and to try and ensure that visitors enter the water safely.

Love Letter to Hawai'i

Chapter Nineteen

My Favorite Aspects of Kona and The Big Island

After providing you with all the information about why it's so expensive to live here, why it's hard to find a job, what kind of pests we have, and so on, I DO want to share with you some of the reasons most of us DO love it here, and why you will want to call Kona and the Big Island home!

Varied Climates

Hawai'i Island contains perhaps the world's greatest concentration of climate types in its 4,038 square miles. From dry, coastal, desert strand; to some of the wettest spots on earth; to hot, humid, tropical lushness; to stark, barren, snow-capped mountains; our big island offers an astonishing array of climates. The varied climates and landscapes were one of our deciding factors on why we chose this island over the others. We wanted to avoid "island fever" and we have! Of course, most tourists come for the beaches, and stay stuck to their beach chairs with their coolers. However, if you are adventurous, like we are, discovering each climate zone will be a fun ride. Speaking of rides, my husband actually bought and tricked out a Toyota 4WD to discover the island! From snowboarding at the top of Mauna Kea, to hiking through the Kona cloud forest in Koloko, to learning about the *Wili Wili* tree on a lava field, the terrain and climates keep the Big Island exciting. Learn more about our climate zones on the Hawai'i Forest and Trail website at:
http://bit.ly/ClimateZones

Scented flowers and Leis

Most people remember Hawai'i for how it smells, especially if they were drenched in the tropical scent of flowers when someone placed a lei around their neck. During the late spring and summer, you can smell the pungent perfume of the plumeria in the air, and witness the varied colors of this fragrant tree. Other flowers you may find in *leis* and in landscaped grounds around Hawai'i are tuberose, gardenia, *pī kake*, and ginger. Each flowering plant has its own interesting story, origin, and place in Hawaiian culture or history. Learn more at this link about which flowers are indigenous, endemic, introduced by Polynesians, Europeans, or other settlers:

http://bit.ly/PopularLeiFlowers

One of my favorite things about living here is running in the morning and having to stop to enjoy the intoxicating smell of the flowers!

Crazy Beautiful Plants

When I first saw a rainbow eucalyptus, I had to run my hands over it and peel away some of the bark to see how a painting could exist on a tree. Have you seen the hula girl hibiscus or just about any type of hibiscus? The native yellow hibiscus is Hawai'i's state flower and really symbolizes the beauty of the natural world in Hawai'i. The vast array of orchids grown on this island is also amazing. Hawai'i Island is also known as Orchid Isle because of all the orchid farms on the east side of the island. The jade ivy and heliconia are nature's work of art, with their extraordinary colors and shapes. If you want to see a bevy of tropical plants, take a trip to Hilo's Botanical Gardens.

http://bit.ly/HiloBotanicalGardens

If you want to see just about every kind of palm tree, fern, and bamboo, plus the rainbow eucalyptus, book a tour of the Kona Cloud Forest Sanctuary.

http://bit.ly/KonaCloudForestSanctuary

We are blessed with an abundance of gorgeous plants all over this island.

Unbelievable Sunsets

For anyone who follows my "365 Things to Do in Kona" Facebook page, you will see that I consistently post Kona sunset photos. Why? Because I can't help but pick up my iPhone to capture another glorious end of the day as the sun dips below the horizon and leaves a fiery presence behind to light up the clouds. Every night is a different canvas. If you spend time here, you will notice two things about our sunsets: The VOG makes the sunsets turn red on the horizon, and it creates some of the most artistic sunsets. You may also see a "green flash" at the moment the sun dips into the ocean. Green flashes occur because the atmosphere can cause the light from the sun to separate out into different colors. Really the best time to see this natural phenomenon is when there are no clouds near the horizon. The walls, balconies, and lanais of the entire downtown area are filled with tourists and residents waiting to capture this sight when the sky is clear at sunset.

Underwater Marine Life

The Big Island, and West Hawai'i in particular, have been noted for having some of healthiest coral reefs in the world, along with clear water, as no above-ground streams flow into the ocean near Kona. Our water is achingly blue on sunny days, and is another reason I moved here. The clear blue water makes swimming, snorkeling, and diving in West Hawai'i an "if I could do this every day, I would" event. Recently, I had a few hours before a client meeting, so I went for a quick snorkel near White Sands Beach, and found myself surrounded by a school of two-foot needlefish, with their leader measuring at least three feet long. I hung out with them for a while and then went to hover above a school of yellow tang. (The yellow tang was so abundant that Kona was nicknamed the "Gold Coast" because tourists would see the flashes of bright yellow all over the reef system when they first flew in. Concerned residents are working hard to stop the collecting of our tropical reef fish.) I had to drag myself away from that reef to get to my meeting, but I was in a state of bliss for hours after that experience.

Our coral is a local source of pride and so, I say again, please do not step on it while you are out in the water.

Hula

Hula is a dance created by the Polynesians celebrating the Hawaiian culture, and is a form of storytelling. It is also deeply spiritual and it takes years not only to learn how to perform a dance, but to know the meaning behind each move. My daughter has learned, in her hula classes at her school, that hula is an avenue to learning the culture and history of the Hawaiians. She has also discovered the precision, patience, practice, and pride the *Kumus* (teachers) instill in their students. Knowing how difficult it is makes watching a performance that much more meaningful. The true masters are amazing to watch. Check out the annual Merrie Monarch Festival in Hilo each May to watch some of the world's best hula performers enchant the audience.

Everyone has a different reason to find the Big Island alluring. Many say our white, gray, black, and green sand beaches are the draw. Some just enjoy being in a place where the temperature, at least near the ocean, does not change more than thirteen degrees year-round, which makes sitting under a palm tree, watching the fronds sway in the breeze, pretty amazing. Personally, I see something amazing every day here, which helps counteract the high cost of calling Hawai'i home.

The Lifestyle

People do not just get up one day and move to the middle of the ocean to sit around watching sunsets. They come for a new and interesting way to live and enjoy their lives. Living life in Kona is amazing. Yes, you may have to work a bit "smarter than the average mainland bear," but the rewards are worth it. Just driving down the road and being able to see the ocean is a reward. Getting up and hearing the birds singing, smelling the tropical perfumed air, being warm all year long, putting on your shorts and a T-shirt day after day, and being surrounded by health-minded, happy people who are not in a rush to get by or in front of you, is a blessing . . . Each . . . Day!

When you are done with work, or on weekends, you can go jump in the ocean and in your mind you get to yell, "I live in Hawai'i!!!" That is one of my favorite things. Sometimes I just yell it out loud. It's okay as those around me (who live here, too) gives me a smile, high five, or a shaka.

Chapter Twenty

The Power of Pele

I would be remiss if I wrote a book about moving to Kona and left out the importance Pele plays on Hawai'i Island. Pele is the Hawaiian goddess of the volcano; her traditional home is Halema'uma'u, the fire pit of Kilauea crater, which has flowed consistently since 1983. Pele has many legends attached to her name and many stories about how this fiery goddess became the main deity in the Hawaiian island chain. http://bit.ly/StoryofPele

One of the most interesting things I have found is that Pele is virtually unknown anywhere else in Polynesia. She is an entity of spiritual power only in the Hawaiian Island chain. And is revered by those on the Big Island, where her power is on display daily.

If you do a web search of Hurricane Iselle (the Category One hurricane that turned into a tropical depression that hit our island on August 8th, 2014) and add in the word "Pele," you will find quite a few videos, photos, and essays about the power of Madame Pele against the force of both Iselle and her brother Julio, the second hurricane that was supposed to hit our island close behind. If you look at video images, you will see that as soon as the storm approached the center of the island, it broke apart and "flung Iselle back into the Pacific from whence she came and scared Julio and made him run to the north," as a local essayist so eloquently opined. Long-time residents of West Hawai'i believe that Pele, along with her creations, 13,000 foot Mauna Loa and Mauna Kea, have the power to protect the island from oncoming storms. After living in Kona through three hurricanes and not getting much of a wind gust and only a bit of a downpour, I am a believer that our lovely island is an amazing deflector of powerful storms.

There are many spiritual residents who believe they are helping Pele by using their conscious power to help push the storms away.

I have to tell you this because if you get to know folks who have been on the West side of the island for any length of time, they will tell you that Pele protects the island, and so does a very powerful spiritual community. Whether you believe it or not, it's useful to know—and think about this . . . King Kamehameha's palace, in downtown Kona, is still standing there after tsunamis, earthquakes, volcanic flows, and hurricanes.

If you live here, or if you visit Hawai'i only once, the one myth of Pele that you will likely hear and should pay attention to is the one surrounding the curses she inflicts on those who remove lava rocks from her island home. While many—including some *Kama'āina* (local residents)—believe that it is only legend, to this day thousands of pieces of lava rocks are mailed back to the island from travelers all over the world, who insist they've suffered bad luck and misfortune as a result. I saw this in person when I was visiting the Kona-Kohala Chamber of Commerce and there were packages of rocks on one of the desks. I asked about it and the marketing person said they get these packages sent to them ALL THE TIME from people who have visited Hawai'i and just want to remove "the bad juju" they experienced after coming home with lava. This is an act of *Ho'pono'pono* (asking for forgiveness). If there is nothing to the power of Pele, why are people doing this each month?

Another power attributed to Pele is that she decides if you will succeed here. If you come and find favor with Pele, you will stay on the island and enjoy your time here. If you come, and your energy and that of Pele's does not mesh, you may find it hard to find and keep a job, find a sense of community, and feel that Kona is HOME. Pele may test you for the first year to see if you really have what it takes to call Hawai'i home. My advice? Come with an open heart, good energy, a sense of wonder and *Aloha*, and do something good for the island while you are here.

I was reading online for more historical information about Pele, and someone wrote in the comments of one detailed blog post: "This does not tell me about Pele at all." It probably does not because to understand Pele, you have to feel her. There is a definitely something deep and powerful on this island and it draws people here. I know this, in part, because of the many times I have heard people say they felt "called to live here."

When I was growing up and living in San Jose, California, I can tell you that not one new resident of San Jose, or the entire Santa Clara County, had ever told me they were called to live there. Now, with the tech boom, I am sure there are people around the world who may say that about being pulled into the promise of Silicon Valley—but that's a different draw. What is the draw to moving and living in Kona? It's not the money. It's the energy.

I wish you the best of luck in your possible move to Kona.

A hui hou!

Meet The Author

Julie Ziemelis

A Silicon Valley escapee, Julie Ziemelis started sharing information about Kona in 2010 on her blog, 365Kona.com, and on her "365 Things to Do in Kona" Facebook page, where she shares photos, videos, and information daily.

Ms. Ziemelis wrote *How to Move to Kona* after being continually asked (via her blogs) about what it takes to make a successful move to Kona and advice on how to live in West Hawaii.

Using insight she has gained from buying real estate, owning her own marketing consultancy business, living in Kona since 2005, raising a family, and coaching new residents in Kona, Ms. Ziemelis offers candid and helpful advice.

Julie doing one of the things she likes to do whereever she goes . . .
a handstand!

22334641R10076

Made in the USA
Middletown, DE
27 July 2015